The Modern Caribbean Economy, Volume I

The Modern Caribbean Economy, Volume I

Alternative Perspectives and Policy Implications

Edited by
Nikolaos Karagiannis
Debbie A. Mohammed

BEP BUSINESS EXPERT PRESS

First published in 2017 by
Business Expert Press, LLC
222 East 46th Street, New York, NY 10017
www.businessexpertpress.com

ISBN-13: 978-1-63157-554-9 (paperback)
ISBN-13: 978-1-63157-555-6 (e-book)

Business Expert Press Economics Collection

Collection ISSN: 2163-761X (print)
Collection ISSN: 2163-7628 (electronic)

Cover and interior design by S4Carlisle Publishing Services
Private Ltd., Chennai, India

First edition: 2017

10 9 8 7 6 5 4 3 2 1

Printed in the United States of America.

Abstract

Caribbean economies have been faced with mounting challenges arising from the increasing pace of economic globalization. The financial crisis of 2007 further exacerbated economic instability due to high foreign debt, lack of competitiveness, declining productivity, and high unemployment and underemployment. This in turn has precipitated increasing social and environmental problems, including poverty, inequality, crime and violence, and environmental degradation, all of which require new perspectives and policy approaches for transformative change and sustainable development. In the 2-volume multidisciplinary edited book **The Modern Caribbean Economy**, Volume I: *Alternative Perspectives and Policy Implications* provides scholars and practitioners with alternative theoretical perspectives and concrete policy recommendations, while Volume II: *Economic Development and Public Policy Challenges* discusses economic, industrial, and social problems facing the Caribbean along with pragmatic proposals to successfully deal with these, while building local resilience and enhancing institutional strength in the region.

Keywords

Caribbean; volatility; economic development; development strategies; public policy; institutional reforms

Contents

Acknowledgements

Our task would have been incomplete if we had not acknowledged those who kindly aided us in completing these two edited volumes. We thank the distinguished contributors for their willingness to participate and to respond to our suggestions, and the executives, advisors, and staff of the Business Expert Press who have provided excellent support throughout the preparation of this project.

We would also like to thank the editorial offices of *Social and Economic Studies* (SES), for kindly permitting revised sections of the article "Boosting the Industrial Competency and Market Development of Caribbean Firms: The Challenge of the Developmental State Approach" (first published in SES vol. 62: 1&2, June 2013) to appear in chapter 2 of Volume I and Volume II, and *Worldwide Hospitality and Tourism Themes* (WHATT) for kindly permitting a slightly amended version of the paper "Crime, Criminal Activity and Tourism Performance: Issues from the Caribbean" (first published in WHATT vol. 4: 1, January 2012) to be included as chapter 3 in Volume II.

Last, but not the least, we would like to thank our families for their continuous encouragement and support, and our colleagues and students for the inducements. We owe them more than we can recount.

Introduction

Setting the Context

The Caribbean is a distinctive socioeconomic order determined by experiences of a historical formation rooted in colonialism and the plantation system, and all the consequences manifested in social stratification, cultural contradictions, and endemic economic limitations. As a result, the persistence of "plantation variables" is a fact, and the economies of the region eventually evolved typically into monocrop production, which is mostly foreign-owned and export-oriented. Later on, since the 1960s, emphasis on crops such as sugar, coffee, and bananas has been replaced by an excessive emphasis on tourism, which has been heralded as the road to modernity and prosperity.

Recently, even though Caribbean countries are signatories to a wide variety of Conventions and international agreements, economies and societies in the region, and all over the world, are grappling with the challenges of globalization and the tyranny of financialization: the astonishing pace of technological innovation, widening poverty gaps, food shortages, climate change, rising energy costs, environmental problems, global financial crises, and vexing social ills such as unemployment and underemployment, rising criminality, health and educational challenges, and the like.

Theoretically, debates concerning "holistic development" (a "holistic" approach utilizes four pillars of sustainability: social, cultural, environmental, and economic) and globalization reveal sharply different views of the new world order. Proponents of current forms of globalization (generally termed "neoliberal" or "corporate") tend to speak in very positive terms, making bold promises about the future. They contend that policies of freer trade and minimally regulated markets will result in high levels of economic growth throughout the world. This growth will in turn lead to broad improvement in living conditions as "a rising tide lifts all boats."

From a neoliberal perspective, globalization is an economically driven process that should proceed on first principles of private property and unrestricted market forces. Regulation should have as its primary—if not sole—function to facilitate and protect private ownership and the "free" operation of supply and demand among producers and consumers. Other economic rules and institutions are "political interferences" that undermine market efficiency and, therefore, should be reduced to a minimum. With a combination of privatization, liberalization and deregulation, globalization should bring maximum prosperity, liberty, democracy, and peace to the whole of humankind.

Neoliberal doctrine has exerted a powerful hold on governing circles during the past quarter-century of accelerated globalization. Faith in free market outcomes has formed the core of the so-called Washington consensus on economic policies (Williamson, *Latin American Adjustment: How Much Has Happened?*, 1990). The early 1990s was even a period for its champions to announce "the end of history" and that "there is no alternative" –no other model but capitalism and liberal democracy seemed possible (Fukuyama, *The End of History and the Last Man*, 1992). In reality, however, only a few select indicators like those related to cross-border trade, direct investment, and permanent migration support the claim that recent growth in world relations is a rerun of earlier history (UNCTAD various reports; UNRISD various papers).

Yet, different critics of current forms of globalization see it differently. They draw attention to links between past and present global economic realities and policies, and point out negative consequences such as vexing levels of inequality, rising debts and debt crises, widespread hunger and poverty, the massive displacement of small farmers and disappearance of small businesses, sweatshop working conditions, the breakdown of community, increased social conflicts, and several ecological crises. According to radical arguments (e.g., David Harvey, William Tabb, and Robert Went, among others), current policies need to be viewed in the context of the overall history and dynamics of the world capitalist system.[1]

The goal of neoliberal policies is to accelerate capital accumulation, with all the side effects of exploitation, concentration of wealth, inequality, and other negative features that this process typically entails. For example, Went (2000: 6), argues that policies of neoliberal globalization are leading to

> a more and more pervasive dictatorship of the market [system]; to greater social inequality as the result of a dual polarization process, both within countries and on a world scale among different countries; to progressive leveling down of wages, working conditions, and social security; to extensive migratory flows; to life-threatening ecological deterioration and destruction; to a greater role for unaccountable international institutions and regional entities; and to further whittling-away of democracy.

Besides, grassroots critics express a much deeper appreciation of ecology, and local cultures and values.[2]

Evidently, globalization has already impacted the economies and societies of the Caribbean: exacerbation of economic instability, rising current account and fiscal deficits alongside high debt obligations, a slowdown in productivity growth, limited adjustment in traditional sectors, high unemployment and underemployment, the reduction and deterioration in public services, the degradation of the environment and natural resources, increasing social problems including crime and violence, the growing distance between rich and poor, and unfair competition arrangements which put Caribbean nations in a situation of ever increasing inferiority. Besides, the nature of the current financial integration of Caribbean countries has created new forms of external vulnerability. As the effects of globalization will more likely intensify, and given its complexity and its potentially disruptive power together with its opportunities, there is clearly an urgent need to understand it, to take advantage of whatever benefits it offers, and to minimize potentially negative outcomes.

The Caribbean has also several strengths as regards globalization: the region is democratic; adheres to a system of laws; has embraced economic liberalism, particularly since the beginning of the 1990s; has a relatively high level of education compared with other less-developed countries; and is mostly English-speaking and geographically close to the USA, the largest single market in the world (UN, *Global E-Government Readiness Report*, 2004). Consequently, the question that arises is: what are realistic development options for Caribbean territories given the policy space available to their national institutions at present?

Clearly, a positive, realistic, and forward-looking stance will not be possible without a good understanding of this new world order which is shaping, and will continue to shape the contemporary Caribbean and the rest of the world. In this era of neoliberal globalization and financialization, however, we would find that there has been little of worth contributed to the concrete task of working out thorough strategies and consistent policies (i.e., an effective local response) for coping with these socioeconomic problems in the Caribbean. Indeed, it is vexing how little attention has been paid to developing rational strategies and pragmatic policies aimed at providing a planning frame to deal with the multidimensional problems of the region.

The multidisciplinary edited book *The Modern Caribbean Economy* consists of two volumes. The first volume appears with the subtitle *Alternative Perspectives and Policy Implications*, and the second with the subtitle *Economic Development and Public Policy Challenges*. Both volumes provide much-needed alternative theoretical notions and offer concrete policy recommendations to national and regional institutions as well as the local business community while engaging scholars, policy makers, professionals, students, and all persons interested in the burning issues associated with these themes. This thorough information is what Caribbean policy makers actually need.

The Structure of Volume I

The edited volume *The Modern Caribbean Economy: Alternative Perspectives and Policy Implications* discusses alternative theoretical views and holistic development-promoting policy considerations aimed at advancing the region's local economies while taking into consideration the impact of globalization and the current crisis. With important contributions by distinguished academics, the manuscript evaluates past efforts and policies, criticizes failed perspectives, and offers alternative strategies, policies, and realistic options to the region's current socio-economic impasse and misery from a distinctly Caribbean viewpoint. Although different areas of concern are addressed, the chapters are informed, to a greater or lesser extent, by such important factors as historical legacy, the role of institutions (including market and government), geopolitics and the international environment, local culture and social psychology, which stand in contrast to the starry-eyed analysis of the current orthodoxy. Overall, the contributions to this edited book not only expand the body of knowledge but, more importantly, provide a rich menu for alternative strategies and policies related to Caribbean endogenous development aspects in the twenty-first century.

Volume I consists of four chapters. Considering that this era of neoliberal globalization and financialization challenges old-fashioned areas of intellectual concern to discovery, explanation and theory, these chapters lay special emphasis on alternative theoretical views aimed at a better understanding of the nature of modern economic realities in the region. They include important analyses such as the possible influence of Canadian staples theory on the Caribbean political economy, main notions of a distinctively Caribbean egalitarian developmentalist framework, modern government capacity requirements, and challenges to improving Caribbean educational systems.

In the opening chapter, Madjd-Sadjadi argues that the plantation economy literature is an outgrowth of Canadian "staples theory" with new packaging, which was married to the existing work of Arthur Lewis. Therefore, according to the author, Canadian political economic insight ought to be included in the history of the development of the Caribbean plantation economy literature. In chapter 2, Karagiannis and Polychroniou describe the historic impact of colonialism on the Caribbean development, cautiously make the case for centralized political involvement in industrial expansion in the era of neoliberal globalization, and propose essential themes and notions towards framing an alternative egalitarian development paradigm for the region. Chapter 3 by Minto-Coy and Berman assesses the past performance of the public sector in the Caribbean context. Taking into consideration vexing challenges, modern demands, and expectations associated with the region's developing states, the authors specify key areas for improving and strengthening their capacity for governance. Finally, in chapter 4, Pearson claims that Caribbean systems of education experience some of the same challenges as many of its global neighbors. The author advocates for critical theory approaches to quality school leadership, which can effectively address these multidimensional challenges.

Our task would have been incomplete if we had not acknowledged those who kindly aided us in completing this edited volume. We thank the distinguished contributors for their willingness to participate and respond to our suggestions, and the advisors and staff of the Business Expert Press who have provided excellent support throughout the preparation of this manuscript. We would also like to thank the editorial offices of *Truthout* and *Social and Economic Studies* (SES) for kindly permitting revised paragraphs of the paper "Boosting the Industrial Competency and Market Development of Caribbean Firms: The Challenge of the Developmental State Approach" (first published in SES vol. 62: 1&2, June 2013) to appear in the second chapter of this book. Last, but not the least, we would like to thank our families for their continuous encouragement and support, and our colleagues and students for the inducements. We owe them more than we can recount.

Nikolaos Karagiannis Debbie A. Mohammed
Winston-Salem, North Carolina, USA
and St. Augustine, Trinidad & Tobago
January 2016

Notes

1. See: Robert Went (2000), *Globalization: Neoliberal Challenges, Radical Responses* (London: Pluto); William Tabb (2001), *The Amoral Elephant: Globalization and the Struggle for Social Justice in the Twenty-First Century* (New York: Monthly Review Press).
2. These categories of radical and grassroots critics are not mutually exclusive as some critics could appropriately be placed in both categories.

CHAPTER 1

The Contribution of Canadian Economic Thought to Caribbean Political Economy

A Preliminary Investigation

Zagros Madjd-Sadjadi

Summary

Chapter 1 seeks to investigate whether there are common theoretical threads between Canadian economic thought and Caribbean political economy. In doing so, the author briefly discusses the "staples theory," the work of Arthur Lewis, the Plantation school literature, and contributions by Eric Williams and William Demas. The author then identifies key points of commonality and disagreement between the different approaches, and concludes with a discussion as to why the Canadian connection was dropped and the Lewis connection was downplayed.

Introduction

When I first stepped foot on the campus of The University of the West Indies, Mona as a newly appointed Lecturer of Economics back in 2003, I entered a storied place steeped in tradition. Here was a university that had produced not one, but two, Nobel laureates, including one in economics, Sir William Arthur Lewis, and I was about to join an illustrious company of scholars who had once roamed these fabled halls from the aforementioned Nobel laureate to such giants in Caribbean economic thought as William Demas, Norman Girvan, George Beckford, Kari Levitt, and Lloyd Best, these latter three thinkers forming the genesis of what had become known as the "plantation economy school" of political economy.

Yet, upon first reading the writings of the "plantation economy school" of political economy formulated at The University of the West Indies, Mona, I was struck that it did not appear to be an indigenous literature at all but bore striking resemblance to the work of Canadian staples theory scholars, such as Harold Innis, Mel Watkins, and, interesting enough, Kari Levitt, in her incarnation as a Canadian scholar who produced the classic work, *Silent Surrender* (1970). The more I looked, the more Canadian connections I saw. Not only was the economic theory similar to that of the staples theorists of Canada but they used similar terminology and each member of the plantation economy school had a notable connection to Canada, with four of them having studied or otherwise worked in the country *prior to* or *contemporaneously with* producing their seminal works and the fifth having worked extensively with Kari Levitt. Yet, importantly, no reference to the work of Canadian scholars was found in the plantation economy school literature. I discovered that this was not the only failure to acknowledge those who had come before because much of the time they either failed to acknowledge or openly denigrated Sir William Arthur Lewis contributions to their theory, despite many connections to that theory. For this latter insight, I am indebted to the work of Mark Figueroa (1998), a fellow economist at The University of the West Indies, who has outlined much of these issues in far more detail than I have attempted in the third section of this essay.

In this essay, I will demonstrate that the plantation economy literature is an outgrowth of Canadian "staples theory" with new packaging, which was married to the existing work of Sir Arthur Lewis, Nobel laureate in economics and the quintessential Caribbean economist of the pre-plantation economy school era. The decision, whether it was overt or unconscious, to fail to acknowledge the Canadian legacy has more to do with the politics of the region than anything else. This is not to articulate a position that the plantation economy research does not have unique, important, and fundamentally original contributions. Nothing could be further from the truth. Instead, it simply is an attempt to state that the intellectual founders owe a debt of gratitude to more than those whom they initially acknowledged. In the next section, I provide a brief discussion of staples theory as envisioned by Harold Innis and new staples theory, which has as its major proponents Mel Watkins and Kari Levitt, and which merges staples theory with other forms of dependency theory to support a non-Marxian foreign-ownership model of the economy. I then examine the work of Sir Arthur Lewis and his contributions to the political economy of the region, especially his groundbreaking works *Theory of Economic Growth* and *Economic Development with Unlimited Supplies of Labour*. This is followed by a discussion of the Plantation economy school literature of George Beckford, Lloyd Best, and Kari Levitt, as well as its supposed development from the work of Raul Prebisch, Eric Williams, and William Demas. During this discussion, I will identify key points of commonality and disagreement between the three approaches under examination. I conclude the paper with a discussion as to why the Canadian connection was dropped and the Lewis connection was downplayed.

Staples Theory

Staples theory is both a theory of regional equilibrium and regional disequilibrium. In the former context, as discussed by the Economic Council of Canada (1977), the theory reduces down to a form of neoclassical trade theory, wherein spatial distribution of resources leads to comparative advantages such that certain regions end up providing raw materials (the hinterland) while the metropoles (the heartland) end up acting as processors of these raw materials not because they lacked the processing power but rather because they possessed the ability to package and get production to market through access to seaways and other transportation networks. According to this theory, the various boom-bust periods of the Canadian hinterlands correspond roughly to changes in economic demand for those goods and the ability of these regions to extract these resources in a competitive fashion. The collapse of the Atlantic fisheries market due to overfishing and inadequate property rights led directly to the dependency of that region on the rest of Canada. The solution is to allow markets to play themselves out properly, having individuals shift their place of employment and residence to areas of more suitable financial suitability. In other words, it is a theory that stresses *people prosperity* over *place prosperity*. Its greatest defender is Courchene (1986) who argues that regional disparities persist because of an inability to separate out these two concepts. Essentially, regional adjustment assistance acts as a form of interprovincial "welfare" that anchors individuals into a particular location, making them less likely to move. While textbooks discuss wage and price flexibility, the real world is one of wage rigidity due to minimum wage legislation, unemployment insurance, and federal policies that provide aid to specifically targeted groups (such as fishermen) to encourage them not to migrate. This is precisely the wrong strategy according to the viewpoint. Courchene (1986: 49) goes out of his way to state, "It would be absurd to argue that the provinces deliberates chose this option. Likewise it would be inappropriate to asset that it was a conscious policy decision on Ottawa's part to generate the current status quo with respect to the economic viability of various provinces." However, if this is the case, one wonders why it is that supposedly rational governments could not foresee the consequences of their actions. To argue that a province that is in a position of dependency will not attempt to maximize its own gains from that condition rather than make a (futile) attempt to break free of the chains appears to be an attempt to derive a politically correct stamp on the logical (but undesirable) natural conclusion.

This form of staples theory coincides with the perspective of the Rowell-Sirois Commission (1940) that sees the extraction of natural resources as one of several stages in economic growth that would eventually result in an economy that no longer is tied to the land. Essentially, the argument is that resource extraction provides the necessary income for capital accumulation that will allow the nation to move up the chain of industrialization to the next stage. This is a lovely sentiment but wholly unsupported by facts, which indicate that Canada is still in many ways more like the resource extraction economy of its past than an advanced industrialized economy of Europe's present. Although Canada has moved up the resource base from fur trade, fisheries, and timber to oil sands, uranium, and potash, it still has a long way to go to become the processing giant that the United States, Europe, or Asia is. In some ways, having resources provides one with the "resource curse", even if it is a relatively benign affliction of it.

In contrast to the equilibrium model depicted above, Harold Innis, in *The Fur Trade in Canada*, provides a decidedly *disequilibrium* model of the economy and is, in fact, the precursor to modern dependency theory, of which the Plantation School play a part. Innis was an economic historian trained in the American Institutionalist school tradition to look at how economic structures determine our destiny. In his book, *A History of the Canadian Pacific Railway* (Innis 1923, 294), he alleged that the exporting for the Canadian prairie provinces of wheat, a staple crop, grown under conditions of pure competition but that were transported by a veritable monopoly in the Canadian Pacific Railroad created the basis for exploitation of the region: "The question as to whether the prairie provinces shall control their own natural resources has become increasingly difficult . . . the dominance of eastern Canada over western Canada seems likely to persist." Similarly, in his books, *The Cod Fisheries* (1940) and *The Fur Trade in Canada* (1930) the locus of control that exists was always in the hands of the dominant powers that could wield monopoly power over the staple producers. This dichotomy would play a central role for Innis in the development of the new Canadian economy:

> The economic history of Canada has been dominated by the discrepancy between the center and margin of western civilization. Energy has been directed towards the exploitation of staple products and the tendency has been cumulative. The raw material supplied to the mother country stimulated manufacturers [in the mother country] of the finished product and also of the products that were in demand in the economy. (Innis 1956c: 385)

In other words, Canada, being a staples producer for the main country, found itself in a peculiar position. As its comparative advantage lay in its ability to produce natural resources in a competitive environment, there would not be a surplus gained to allow it to develop the same level of industry as was found in Europe. This could lead to one of three different possible scenarios. The first was an outgrowing of the original staples economy. It was this view that was undertaken by W. A. Macintosh

(1964) who would argue, similar to Rostow's (1960) *Stages Theory of Industrialization*, that staples production was but a necessary first step in a transition to a full-fledged manufacturing power. However, this could only occur if diversification around the economic staple could be sufficient to catapult the economy to the next level. For example, Ontario began as a producer of wheat and barley. To get these commodities to the market, it developed transportation linkages and the servicing of these linkages allowed the economy to develop an infrastructure necessary to move industrial goods. At the same time, due to its control over transportation linkages and the reduced costs associated with generating small industrial production in the area due to the proximity of this infrastructure allowed the creation of a nascent industrial economy, which later grew into the powerhouse that it is today. However, much of this can also be attributed to import substitution that was carried out under the nationalization policies of various Canadian governments. Thus Canada, through import substitution was able to grow industrially. However, this did not alleviate the natural geographic issues initially found with staples production. Instead, it merely transferred to the industrial heartland of the country the same role that had previously been occupied by the mother country of England, while the staples-producing hinterlands continued to act as economic dependencies. Innis argued that we could not simply take for granted what had transpired in Europe because one could not "fit the phenomena of new countries into the economic theories of old countries" (Innis 1956a: 10).

Innis begins his tale by noting that many of the staples that were produced, all of which were unprocessed at least at first in the country of extraction, were not subject to free competition. The Hudson Bay Company was created for the explicit purpose of supplying fur to England. It was granted a monopoly trading permit to engage in this activity and demand for the product was a derived demand based upon the manufacturing of fur clothes in England. Since the furriers had already set up extensive manufacturing facilities and the new found colony had neither a transportation network nor a large population of Europeans at the time, the tendency would be to ship these products back to England for eventual manufacturing. Canada grew in population predominantly by immigration and, therefore, it would not have the industrial capabilities of the mother country. The reason for this was two-fold. Industrialization required a large population to be moved from off the land into factories and this was simply not available in Canada. Second, industrialization was quite advanced relative to another that could be undertaken in Canada during this time so there was little incentive to develop industrial capabilities given that the major market for these goods was the mother country. It made little difference whether one was to produce in the colony or in the home country, since very little of the output of the colony would go to service the colonial population. Therefore, there would be little incentive to create manufacturing plants. It was only when the population became large enough to support its own manufacturing that such endeavors became reasonable and the tendency was then to locate such plants in what would be the industrial heartland due to transportation linkages.

Thus, staple production created the impetus for more immigration and whether industry would be set up tended to depend on the nature of the staple itself. The gathering of cod, for example, caused the development of secondary industries supporting the development of fisheries, such as shipbuilding. Production of wheat led to railroads, barges, and production of grains and cereals. Staples also defined the characteristics of the society with fishery-based economies having less centralization than agricultural-based economies since the latter's products had to be moved to rail lines that were permanently positioned:

> Concentration on the production of staples for export to more highly industrial areas in Europe and later in the U.S. had broad implications for the Canadian economic, political, and social structure. Each stable, in turn left its stamp, and the shift to a new staple invariably produced periods of crises. (Innis 1956b: 8)

This transformation from one staple to another was a second possible avenue of adjustment. As technology and tastes changed, so too would the staple production. Lobster production, for example, which is now a major source of fisheries income in the North Atlantic had no major basis until the start of this century as the delicacy was regarded more as suitable for the likes of orphans and prisoners. Lobster meat was used as fertilizer in the Maritimes up until the turn of the last century. This ended with the development of modern transportation that allowed the lobster to be sold live in faraway ports. The denigration of taste that occurred in the canning process was alleviated and the commodity became much more valuable. This is one way that staples producing economies can survive, by adapting and changing with the times.

The third possibility is what is known as the staples trap (Watkins 1963). This is the most pessimistic outlook for the staples economy and occurs when "staples exploitation limited the options and opportunities for a more equitable and controlled distribution of economic development, leading the country invariably deeper and deeper into a 'staples trap' of dependency and stagnation" (Brodie 1990: 42). As prices fall for the staple over time due to competition from other entities or because quantities fall due to over extraction of the staple or because of increases in population that production of the staple can no longer support or because the staple is no longer in such great demand for whatever reason, the country becomes mired in poverty and its dependency on the staple becomes an albatross around its proverbial neck. This tends to occur when backward, forward, and final demand linkages are insufficiently broad to support a higher standard of living or the progression to a new type of economy is no longer dependent on the now outdated staple.

Sir William Arthur Lewis

The only Nobel laureate in economics to have worked in the Caribbean, his work is significantly denigrated by the Caribbean Plantation School theorists. He was born in St. Lucia and was a prominent figure in the development of the West Indies, taking a position at the University College of the West Indies campus in Mona, Kingston, Jamaica as its first Principal from 1958 to 1960 and as the first Vice-Chancellor of the newly formed University of the West Indies, Mona in Kingston, Jamaica from 1960 to 1963. Yet despite his West Indian pedigree, Lloyd Best (1966: 29) argues that Demas deserves credit as having formulated "the first serious contribution of a West Indian economist to the general theory of development," a slighting of the great intellectual thinker that was rampant at the University of the West Indies during the 1960s and 1970s, which "came, not in the form of a critique, but of shifting focus from the work to the personality of the man and attacks on him as an 'Afro-Saxon', etc." (Pantin 1998: 137). Best himself likens this to the notion that "all intellectual generations tend to commit patricide" (Pantin 1998: 138).

The confrontation with Lewis has as much to do with the internal strife at the University of the West Indies, Mona economics department as with anything else. It was Lewis who had placed in the position of Head of Department, the economist Charles M. Kennedy and while a number of West Indian economists were to find their homes at the department in the coming years, a clash of civilizations that occurred in 1964–65 sparked a nerve that was not easily redressed. Although Lewis was no longer with the university, his appointed successor as the Head of Department of Economics was not a man given to identifying with nationalistic jingoism. As George Beckford, one of the Young Turks in the Department would put it, in that year a course on "Caribbean Economic Problems" was proposed. The proposal was put forth by the West Indian economists but their majority opinion was overruled by Professor Kennedy who argued "there were no economic problems specific to the Caribbean and that this proposal, if accepted, would lead eventually to an undesirable state of 'parochialism'" (Beckford as quoted in Levitt 2000: 440).

This antagonism is unfortunate because Lewis forms the first cogent articulation of the plantation economy problem. Essentially, according to Lewis' magnum opus, *The Theory of Economic Growth* (1955), the problem for tropical agricultural producers was the greater productivity in that sector translated into declining terms of trade such that the benefits of increased productivity were granted to the consumer to the detriment of the producer. The major issue that Caribbean economists had with Lewis was his standing as the chief architect of what they believed to be a failed policy of recolonization via foreign ownership and control. Much of these arguments would find articulation in another form in Kari Levitt's influential Innis-inspired text *Silent Surrender: The Multinational Corporation in Canada* (1970). It is a misreading of Lewis to suggest that he supported the introduction of foreign capital over domestic capital when the two were presented as equal choices. The problem is that the individuals needed to lead the problem-solving exercise needed to be developed within the society and that proved difficult in an area where few had been given the opportunity to blossom as managers. He argued that it was better to utilize the resources at home prior to going abroad for assistance (Lewis 1958) but was not averse to going abroad for assistance if such resources were not forthcoming at home.

The problem for Lewis was that foreign investors saw the Caribbean as no different than any other area. As such, unless advances in productivity were translated into a reduction in the base wage per unit produced, capital flight to other areas would occur. Essentially, the reliance on agricultural production and, in later years to other natural resources such as bauxite and petroleum, were such that product differentiation could not occur. Thus the sugar produced in one country was equivalent to that produced anywhere else. Therefore, the lowest cost producer would gain the lion's share of production. There was little incentive to make marked investments in the locality since production costs determined whether one would stay or go. Lewis' (1954) seminal breakthrough was the essay "Economic Development with Unlimited Supplies of Labour" in which he suggests that so long as the commodity being offered is relatively plentiful when compared with demand for it and the commodity can reasonably be produced using only a fraction of the labor available in the area while, at the same time, there are no alternative sources of employment, the limiting factor of scarcity of labor does not apply. As such, increases in productivity are completely offset by declines in the terms of trade. If we wanted to raise cost of sugar, for example, we would have to make it scarce relative to demand. Since this is impossible to accomplish, the burden shifts to the producer to provide the lowest possible cost. Since there are, for the sake of argument, unlimited quantities of labor, wages fall to subsistence levels. The Ricardian "Iron Law of Wages" applies in full force. There is no desire among the capitalist class to invest more heavily in the sector because all such investments will simply result in a lowering of prices and thus capital has no incentive to make the improvements necessary to assist the lot of the peasantry. Indeed, since capital is, in the neo-Ricardian sense, granted a fixed return based on the economy-wide return to capital, additional investments would simply lower that rate of return below that available to other investment opportunities. Therefore, such a policy is not followed:

"Cane sugar production is an industry in which productivity is extremely high by any biological standard. It is also an industry in which output per acre has trebled over the past 70 years—a rate of growth unparalleled by any other major agricultural industry in the world—certainly not by the wheat industry. Nevertheless, workers in the cane sugar industry continue to walk barefooted and to live in shacks, while workers in wheat enjoy among the highest living standards in the world. However vastly productive the sugar industry may become, the benefit accrues chiefly to consumers." (Lewis 1955: 281)

Lewis saw foreign capital as concentrating its efforts on expanding exports in part because the capital was foreign. That it would have a home country bias was noted as far back as Adam Smith. But he also saw that the problem lay in not having sufficient jobs available for the masses. So long as subsistence production was in place alongside export-based production, there would be no rising standard of living. The reasoning was that a capitalist would never have to offer a higher wage because there was always another subsistence farmer willing to work at the subsistence wage. Therefore

. . . so long as productivity is constant in subsistence production, practically all the benefit of increases in productivity in the commercial crops accrues to the consumer and not to the producer. The individual country can benefit by keeping ahead of the average for the tropical world, and will lose if it falls behind; but tropical producers, taken as a whole, do not benefit from higher productivity in commercial crops, so long as productivity remains constant in subsistence food production. Greater productivity is offset by adverse terms of trade. (Lewis 1961, p. xix)

The solution for Lewis was an industrial policy based not on laissez-faire but on state-initiated capitalism designed to provide sufficient employment for the region so as to eliminate the subsistence sector. When such a policy could not be undertaken using domestic capital, one should seek out foreign capital and have that capital harnessed with the explicit requirement that training in such areas as managerial competence and entrepreneurial skill could be manifest in the domestic population rather than allowing the foreign entity to control production processes from abroad.

Plantation Economy School

The Plantation Economy school is generally thought to have sprouted out of the work of Lloyd Best, George Beckford, Kari Levitt and is generally considered to be a form of dependency theory. Dependency theory is thought to have originated with Raul Prebisch's work in the 1950s but a reading of Prebisch indicates that his goals were far different from those of the dependency theorists. Indeed, his central argument mirrors Lewis in that he argued that the terms of trade would decline as technology improves, resulting in the center receiving the bulk of any benefits from advances in technology and trade. Essentially, his was an empirical argument while Lewis made the theoretical connection between this decline and the economic structure that existed in the Caribbean and most of the third world. Prebisch saw the Infant Industry argument made by Frederich List as the savior for the third world and argued for Import Substitution Industrialization (ISI), such that high tariff barriers would be enacted to protect local industry and allow it to fill its home market with goods. By protecting it initially, it would be able to increase its efficiency to such a level that it would eventually be able to thrive. What Prebisch did not account for was the rampant corruption that would find itself throughout the Third World in the form of rent-seeking and the resultant inability of infant industries to ever outgrow their diapers.

It was to be in this context that dependency theory emerged. Unsatisfied with the progress of ISI, dependency theory suggested that non-capitalist forms of production would better suit the progress of nations and many of the scholars came under the allure of Marxian analysis. Certainly, Eric Williams whose seminal work *Capitalism and Slavery* published in the 1940s, was also amenable to the notion that economic dependency had at least partly to do with the capitalist form of production. This does not mean that there was an embracing of the Soviet Union but rather a socialization of activity along nationalistic lines was in order and the calling for change was found throughout Latin America during the late 1960s and early 1970s. The irony was that the Canadian staples theorists were moving in a similar direction with Levitt's (1970) *Silent Surrender*, the *Task Force on Foreign Ownership and the Structure of Canadian Investment*, which was also known as the Watkins (1968) Report, and Lumsden's

(1970) *Close the 49ᵗʰ Parallel etc.: The Americanization of Canada*, all of which argue that Canada was increasingly becoming a dependency of the United States. Canada also found itself with a militant advocacy group for socialism in the form of the Waffle, which was founded in 1969 by leading staples theorists Mel Watkins and James Laxer.

The immediate acknowledged forerunner of the Plantation Economy literature was a book by William G. Demas (1965), then head of the Economic Planning Division of the government of Trinidad and Tobago entitled *The Economics of Development in Small Countries with Special Reference to the Caribbean*. Demas had come to McGill University in 1964 to perform research and deliver a series of lectures that would form the basis of this book. His arrival at the instigation of Kari Levitt is the first clear bridge between Canadian academics and their Caribbean counterparts. Demas' work echoes sentiments of Innis in that he makes special reference to the inability of small countries to pursue large-scale industrialization because of a lack of ability to finance economies of scale. As such, they become dependent on outside forces and, as such, he argues that engaging in customs unions with more advanced countries will only lead them to being marginalized as they will be unable to develop industry on a sufficient scale to generate such economies. He notes, as does Innis, that the conditions found in the Caribbean are different from those found in the small states of Europe when they went through their industrialization phases. He further argues that economic dependence on external sourcing of necessities makes development in the Caribbean particularly difficult. His one major contribution over that found in Canadian staples theory is the notion that small states could integrate themselves and pursue scale economies. As such, he championed the formation of CARICOM and served as its Secretary-General.

About the same time, the New World Group was formed by a group of Caribbean intellectuals and a corresponding similar group was headed in Montreal by Kari Levitt. Levitt (1998: 3) notes that neither she nor Best were well equipped with the Latin American Structuralist/Dependency School theorists at the time:

> I was attracted to the idea of modelling Caribbean economic reality on its own terms, to reveal how such highly open and

dependent economies adjust to the changing fortunes of their commodity export sector; how incomes generated are distributed between foreign and national capital; wage earners and the government; and how employment is generated. The approach was recognizably "structuralist" in the Latin American sense of the term. *But we had read little of the literature* [emphasis added], with the notable exception of Celso Furtado's *Economic History of Brazil.*

She goes on to credit Dudley Seers (1964) for having shone a light on that literature for them. Levitt (1998: 3) notes that while they used the term 'the plantation' for their principal unit of analysis, the plantation really represented all manner of industries that were essentially staples-producing, such as "sugar, bauxite, . . . or petroleum industries" as well as the tourism industry. Like Canada, the Caribbean was in terms of "the leading export sectors and import substitution manufacturing . . . predominantly owned and controlled by foreign capital" (Levitt 1998: 3). Levitt (1998: 8) further notes that the New World Group's principal publication outlet, the *New World Quarterly*, was being published in Montreal and that journal served as the first outlet for what would later become *Silent Surrender.*

Best (1966), who worked with Levitt in Canada from 1966 to 1969, would critique Demas' (1965) conclusions that smallness lead to dependency and argued that societal factors played a role in dependency and, ultimately, a role in eliminating that dependency. The Plantation economy critique is predominantly based on the notion that foreign capital dominates over the society. As such it is little different from the arguments played out by the staples theorists in Canada and the argument that capital seeks cheap labor as opposed to upgrading its productivity is stated thus:

What is the point of incurring the costs of a creative and expensive structural adjustment in the old place when it is so much easier and cheaper to start fresh in an entirely new location? What this means is that there is a built-in process of running down a plantation to the point of decline and collapse (Best 1998: 31)

This is eerily reminiscent of the "staples trap" (Watkins 1963) wherein, to compete, some entities may choose to forgo investment in the hopes of lowering costs but this leads inevitably to a pathway to its destruction:

> The theory of plantation economy therefore not only describes domination and dependence; it exposes the mechanism of mal-distribution of the gains from trade and of persistent poverty or underdevelopment, so misnamed. (Best 1998: 31)

The unique features of the plantation economy literature lie, therefore, not in their prescriptive basis, which tends to mirror their contemporary staples theorists' arguments for nationalization of various industries to escape from foreign ownership issues, but rather their description of the structural characteristics of the Caribbean economies. However, in doing so, the theorists destroy all possibility of generalization in favor of examining the "special case" of the Caribbean. They note that the individuals who run the plantations are tied to the metropole, just as those who ran the staples industries were tied to the industrial heartland or the mother country. With production financed out of other countries, costs were not transparent so "transfer pricing favoring the transfer of surplus to the metropole continues to be a problem whenever a large private enterprise is simultaneously engaged in the production and the overseas marketing of an export commodity" (Levitt 1998: 13–14). This problem harkens back to Innis' objection that staples production was dependent upon the desires of the overseas market and potentially would lead to an underde-velopment of a domestic market.

At the same time, we see the dependency theory school's discussion that this "export bias" would follow from an "*implicit assumption . . . that 'world prices' are the 'right prices' which should determine resource* allocation in all countries [and this leads inevitably to] the *grossly unequal* distribution of purchasing power on a world scale" (Levitt 1998: 14, emphasis as in original).

Finally, we turn to George Beckford, whose 1972 study *Persistent Poverty: Under-development in Plantation Economies of the Third World*, picks up on these themes. Beckford (1972), notes in the introduction to his book, that his "whole view of plantation economy and society has

been profoundly influenced by Lloyd Best." Once again, not a single cita-
tion to Innis is found nor to any other Canadian staples theorist, with
the citing of Levitt's contributions confined to her collaborations with
Best. Beckford traces the plantation economy through its interweavings
of history and society but his manner differs from that of Innis. Rather
than concentrating on geography as the defining characteristic, Beckford
chooses race, on which he goes into considerable detail including the profound problems of once being an enslaved peoples. His work does not
contain the same words that are found in the Canadian staples literature.
Noticeably absent are the words "staples" and "hinterland" that are sprin-
kled throughout the Best and Levitt work. Beckford also does not have
any obvious direct Canadian connection, having spent his sabbatical time
at Stanford University. However, by cutting Beckford off from this rich
and vast literature, the development of the school changed from one focusing on the monocrop to the actual form of production, the plantation.
As such, the development of the plantation school may be considered as
having gone in a different direction than if the original Canadian legacies
had been openly acknowledged.

Conclusion

The history of economic thought is replete with examples of how
non-Western concepts are usurped by the West. Examining the Nobel
Prize in Economics, this Western domination of economic thought appears to be true even in the modern era. At the time of this writing (in
2014), since the founding of the Nobel Memorial Prize in Economics,
there have been 75 winners with only two (Sir Arthur Lewis and Amartya
Sen) having been born or served much of their time in the developing
world.

This would not be a problem if it were not based on Eurocentrism.
Blaut (1993) offers up an interesting analysis of the expansion of European
domination through the myth that progress emanates from the Western
Greco-Roman heritage. Madjd-Sadjadi (2014) notes that the history of
economic thought has an extreme Western bias and points to achievements in economic theory by the Chinese that predate their recognized
Western equivalent concepts by hundreds of years.

Therefore, the development of a truly unique indigenous theory of development growing out of research in the third world should be one that is celebrated, not questioned. However, the problem is that this wonderful fairy tale of overcoming vast limitations in terms of resources to develop a unique and important new theory is exactly that: a fairy tale. Part of the problem can be related by Mamdani (1995: 24) who relates that "Without research, education turns into a consumer product, neither original nor creative, nor inspiring independence of thought." Furthermore, without that independence of thought, without that breaking free of the intellectual chains of the colonial powers, can the formerly colonized ever be truly free?

This is the great conundrum that must be explored when dealing with these issues. It is not so much that there is considerable overlap between the theories of Innis and those of the Caribbean plantation economy writers a generation and a half removed, for Innis sets the tone for the entire dependency school literature. Rather it is that there is no acknowledgment of this linkage by the later writers. This also was true about the linkages to Lewis. Their attitudes towards Lewis, who could not normally be overlooked, serve to help frame the disengagement that they would also find with Innis. The fact that at least one of the formulators of the school was intimately familiar with the Canadian staples thesis should not go unnoticed. For the sole non-West Indian member of the "plantation school" not only was familiar with Innis but Levitt (1970: 46) actually took the time to write in a book that was written contemporaneously with her plantation economy work:

> It seems to have escaped the attention of most of our economists that the insights contained in the writings of the late Harold Innis are highly relevant to an understanding of our contemporary relationship to the United States. The misconception that Innis's staples of fish and fur are an unpalatable diet compared with the elegant apparatus of modern economic theory has deprived recent generations of Canadian economists of the building blocks of a theory of Canadian development.

Even more telling of this linkage, providing the "smoking gun" as it were, that solidifies this connection is the following:

Innis was the chronological antecedent of the Latin American economists in developing a "metropolis-periphery" approach to American
staple economies, and shared with them the attempt to widen the parameters of analysis to comprehend categories which are convention-
ally assumed to lie beyond the strictly economic. (Levitt 1970: 46)

Yet despite this and the recurrent use by plantation economy theorists
of the terms hinterland, heartland/metropoles, and staples that abound in
the Canadian context, but not very often used in the dependency literature,
which usually uses the terms periphery, center, and a variety of terms to describe the resource-based or primary goods production of the Third World,
there appears not one single reference to Innis or Watkins or any other
Canadian staples theorist with the exception of Levitt, whose contributions
are only noted in her work that dwells on the Caribbean or in a peripheral
note regarding her contemporaneous work on Canada that would become
Silent Surrender. The implication was for Caribbean scholars who had not
read her Canadian work that *Silent Surrender* may, in fact, have emanated
out of the work done on the Caribbean and not the other way around.

So it appears that the basis of this was to attempt to establish for the
Plantation School its own footing as a uniquely "Third World" approach
to the problem. If it acknowledged its debt of gratitude to its Canadian
antecedents in the great body of its own work, it would have held its
claims of having been an indigenous solution up for attack. By refusing
to acknowledge that much of it came from elsewhere, it would be more
palatable. Best refused to acknowledge the contributions of Lewis for a
similar reason: Lewis had been instrumental in the postcolonial industrialization process of inviting foreign capital to set up in the Caribbean. Yet,
Best attempted to downplay this by arguing "I know from experience that
the generations inevitably have to murder their fathers to confirm their
adulthood" (Best as quoted by Figueroa 1998: 101).

Figueroa (1998: 102) tends to dismiss as self-serving Best's argument
that his differences with Lewis were methodological and not political:

[Best's] explanation of the school's attitude to Lewis is of little
merit. It is true that in the process of "product differentiation"
new thinkers often tend to focus on their differences with their

predecessors. There are definite imperatives towards excessive ne-
gation, but a central point of this article is that we need to be wary
of the tendency to annihilate our forbearers, leaving ourselves the
poorer for the neglect of their insights.

A similar statement could be made for including Canadian political economic insight in the history of the development of the plantation economy literature.

Notes

1. The "resource curse", first identified by Auty (1993) although discussed in
   the literature in other ways well before that, is the observation that countries
   that have plenty of natural resources end up growing at a slower rate than
   those endowed with nothing. Essentially, the theory behind it is two-fold:
   first, countries with resources lack the incentive to invest in higher productivity enterprises simply because they have a natural opulence and second,
   even when they do end up investing, they do so in a miscalculated manner
   because their revenues appear plentiful during good times and dry up during bad times. In essence fiscal mismanagement leads to their slow growth.
   Reasons for this problem can be found in intrastate conflict (Nigeria),
   high levels of government corruption (Russia) due to a rent-seeking society (Krueger 1974), and exchange rate appreciation due to Dutch disease
   (Corden 1984; Van Wijnbergen 1984), which occurs because high resource
   endowments provide pressures on the exchange rate, raising it to levels
   whereby the manufacturing sectors of a country are no longer competitive.
   The current "petro-dollarification" of the Canadian dollar is an example of
   this latter problem.

References

Auty, Richard M. (1993). *Sustaining Development in Mineral Economies:
The Resource Curse Thesis.* London: Routledge.
Beckford, George (1972). *Persistent Poverty: Underdevelopment in Plantation Economies of the Third World.* Kingston, Jamaica: The University
of the West Indies Press.
Best, Lloyd (1966). "Size and Survival," *New World Quarterly* 2(3): 58–63.
_____ (1998). "Outlines of a Model of Pure Plantation Economy (After
twenty-five years)," *Marronage* 1(1): 27–40.

Blaut, J. M. (1993). *The Colonizer's Model of the World: Geographic Diffusionism and Eurocentric History.* New York: The Guilford Press.

Brodie, Janine (1990). *The Political Economy of Canadian Regionalism.* Toronto: Harcourt Brace Jovanovich, Canada.

Cordon, William M. (1984) "Boom Sector and Dutch Disease Economics: Survey and Consolidation." *Oxford Economic Papers* 36(3): 359–380.

Courchene, Thomas J. (1986). "Avenues of Adjustment: The Transfer System and Regional Disparities" in Donald J. Savoie, ed. *The Canadian Economy: A Regional Perspective.* Toronto: Methuen.

Demas, William G. (1965). *The Economics of Development in Small Countries with Special Reference to the Caribbean.* Montreal: McGill University Press.

Economic Council of Canada (1977). *Living Together: A Study of Regional Disparities.* Ottawa: Minister of Supply and Services.

Figueroa, Mark (1998). "The Plantation School and Lewis: Contradictions, Continuities and Continued Caribbean Relevance," *Marronage* 1(1): 98–123.

Innis, Harold (1923). *A History of the Canadian Pacific Railway.* Toronto: McClelland and Stewart, Ltd.

_____ (1956a). "The Teaching of Economic History in Canada," in M. Q. Innis, ed., *Essays in Canadian Economic History,* Toronto: University of Toronto Press.

_____ (1956b). *Empire and Communication.* Toronto: University of Toronto Press.

_____ (1956c). *The Fur Trade in Canada: An Introduction to Canadian Economic History, Revised Edition.* Toronto: University of Toronto Press.

Krueger, Anne O. "The Political Economy of the Rent-Seeking Society," *American Economic Review* 64(3): 291–303.

Lewis, William A. (1954). "Economic Development with Unlimited Supplies of Labour," Manchester School of Economic and Social Studies 22(2): 139–91.

Lewis, William A. (1955). *The Theory of Economic Growth.* London: Allen and Unwin.

_____ (1958) "Employment Policy in an Underdeveloped Area," *Social and Economic Studies* 7(3): 42–54.

_____ (1961). "Foreword" in Gisela Eisner, *Jamaica 1830–1930: A Study in Economic Growth*. Manchester, England: Manchester University Press.

Levitt, Kari (1970). *Silent Surrender: The Multinational Corporation in Canada*. Toronto: Macmillan Company.

Levitt, Kari Polanyi (1998). "The Plantation Economy Models: My Collaboration with Lloyd Best," *Marronage* 1(1): 1–26.

_____ (2005). *Reclaiming Development: Independent Thought and Caribbean Community*. Kingston, Jamaica: Ian Randall Publishers.

_____ ed. (2000). *The George Beckford Papers*. Kingston, Jamaica: Canoe Press.

Lumsden, Ian. (1970). *Close the 49th Parallel etc.: The Americanization of Canada*. Toronto: University of Toronto Press.

MacIntosh, W. A. (1964) *The Economic Background of Dominion-Provincial Relations*. Toronto: McClelland & Stewart.

Madjd-Sadjadi, Zagros (2014). "China: 2500 Years of Economic Thought," in Vincent Barnett (ed.) *Routledge Handbook of the History of Global Economic Thought*. London: Routledge.

Mamdani, Mamoud (1995). "A reflection on higher education in equatorial Africa: Some lessons for South Africa," *South African Journal of Higher Education* 9(2): 20–7.

Pantin, Dennis A. (1998). "Reflections on the Plantation Economy Conference: Proposals for Economic Research and Teaching at UWI," *Marronage* 1(1): 129–141.

Rostow, W. W. (1960). *The Stages of Economic Growth: A Non-Communist Manefesto*. Cambridge: Cambridge University Press.

Rowell-Sirois Commission (1940). Royal Commission on Dominion-Provincial Relations. Ottawa: King's Printer.

Seers, Dudley (1964). "The Mechanism of an Open Petroleum Economy," *Social and Economic Studies* 13(2): 233–242.

Van Wijnbergen, Sweder (1984). "The 'Dutch Disease': A Disease after All?" *The Economic Journal* 94(373): 41–55.

Watkins, Mel et al. (1968). *Task Force on Foreign Ownership and the Structure of Canadian Industry*. Ottawa: Queen's Printer.

Watkins, Mel H. (1963) "A Staple Theory of Economic Growth." *Canadian Journal of Economics and Political Science* 29(2): 141–158.

CHAPTER 2

Towards a Holistic Development Framework for the Caribbean

Key Theoretical Notions and Policy Implications

Nikolaos Karagiannis and C. J. Polychroniou

Summary

Chapter 2 describes the historic impact of colonialism on the Caribbean development, presents Caribbean development efforts since the end of World War II, cautiously makes the case for institutional political involvement in local industrial expansion in the era of neoliberal globalization, and proposes main themes and notions towards framing an alternative egalitarian development paradigm for the region.

Introduction: The Political Economy of Caribbean Development in Retrospect

Historically, the Caribbean countries developed under the tutelage of different European empires, and more recently under North American dominance. As a result, the Caribbean came to be a classic case of plantation society as there is a certain unity to the region's development and in its patterns of historical evolution. Furthermore, the *plantation economy* models emphasized the historical continuity of the Caribbean dependence from the slave plantation to modification following emancipation, to further modification in the postcolonial era. Political independence established national sovereignty (i.e., "flag independence") in older and newer nations of the Commonwealth Caribbean when both groups were integrated into the international system. Consequently, the political process of national independence converted states, societies, and nations that had evolved as integral parts of the global system. The effect was to legitimize their autonomy based on concepts of self-determination (Payne and Sutton 2001).

In the case of the newer nations, independence coincided with the beginning of a new era that was defined by the decline of the old great powers and the rise of two superpowers with antagonistic ideologies and strategic interests: the United States and the Soviet Union. Main features of the post-World War II global capitalist economy (the creation of a post-World War II global socialist economy was also undertaken by the Soviet Union) were the emergence of the monetary regime of Bretton Woods, with global institutions at its core (the International Monetary Fund and the International Bank for Reconstruction and Development, now known as the World Bank) that were designed to facilitate the incorporation of the developing nations into the global capitalist system via the shaping of the macroeconomic policy of the South; a dramatic increase in the integration of national economies in terms of trade, finance, and foreign direct investment; the emergence of the U.S. dollar as the dominant international currency, which reflected America's hegemonic role in the global capitalist economy; and the rise of a "cooperative-security" organization (NATO) under the aegis of the U.S. whose mission was to protect western capitalism from the perceived threat of Soviet communism.

During the last five decades or so, the region has tried different development models, ranging from industrialization based on imported inputs and technology, to models of structural change which prioritized tourism and other services, to open regionalism which blends regional integration with efforts to boost the export competitiveness of tradable goods and services. However, despite all these models, various strategies and policies have often been conducted with poor rigor on a political level and have repeatedly set Caribbean initiatives up for failure. Evidently, the main

Caribbean trajectory has relied on metropolitan initiatives in investment, technology and marketing, and on continued metropolitan ownership and control of the region's main means of production and domestic demand. The political independence of Caribbean nations has not been accompanied by any significant advancement of their national economies: unbalanced economic structures; international specialization based on unequal exchange; excessive foreign financial and technological penetration; chronic current account deficits; and a dependent monetary system, are among the outstanding features of the Caribbean "blocked development" or "underdevelopment." Largely, foreign decisions determine the growth prospects of Caribbean economies whereas most local resources, natural, human, and technological, remain basically underdeveloped. Therefore, Caribbean economies have been seriously challenged by a lack of indigenous industrial capacity and export competitiveness, which are among the main factors needed for the achievement of sustained growth and endogenous development.

Past Development Efforts

A depiction of Caribbean development efforts since the end of World War II may distinguish four broad phases: the 1950s up to the mid-1960s; the late 1960s and the 1970s; the 1980s; and the 1990s and beyond. The first phase, the 1950s and 1960s, was characterized by the promotion of the modernizing potential of industrialization and economic diversification as a means of overcoming the traditional Caribbean problems of "smallness" and high dependence on agriculture, and created expectations that other economic benefits would also follow. In some countries (e.g., Jamaica and Trinidad), the emergence of modern export industries in the mineral sector was a strong sign of this development thrust (Payne and Sutton 2001: 2–3).

W. Arthur Lewis[1] extensive work on industrialization and his "dual economy model" (1954) in an underdeveloped country provided the theoretical insights underpinning this strategy. He saw industrialization as an essential process for shifting labor into manufacturing, where it is more productive. Consequently, industrialization was expected to help the region overcome the dual problems of markets and resources: the region was short of capital, industrial power was expensive and the available raw material base limited, but wage rates were low by the developed world's standards.

Influenced by Lewis, a number of Caribbean countries developed import substitution policies to facilitate light manufacturing industries. To attract much needed investments by foreign firms, he proposed a package of investment incentives modeled upon the Puerto Rican experience. The inflow of foreign investments would result in higher levels of profits and local savings, and would transmit industrial skills to local people to set in motion self-sustaining growth (Payne and Sutton 2001: 3–4). In the Caribbean, Lewis also addressed issues in education policy and problems of export orientation and political integration.

Lewis policy proposal for industrialization had an immediate impact on newly emerging Commonwealth Caribbean nations as foreign capital responded to the appeals of their governments and flowed in substantial amounts to set up several manufacturing industries. By the late 1960s, manufacturing contributed 15 percent of GDP in Jamaica, 16 percent in Trinidad, 13 percent in Guyana, and 9 percent in Barbados.[2] However, the newly set-up industries were only "final-touch" firms, were based on the assembly of imported inputs, had relatively little local value-added, and generally failed to penetrate export markets. The established industries produced few jobs, had often limited commitment to local development, and were finding it profitable to move their operations to other locations offering new or better options of inducements and conditions. Furthermore, in the 1970s, Caribbean countries faced severe economic difficulties. Therefore, the validity of the Lewis' model of development came increasingly under question in scholarly and political discussions and, in a number of countries, the government was pushed into a position of greater involvement in the management of the economy.

Tourism was the other new sector on which Caribbean nations started placing special emphasis in the 1950s and 1960s. In some islands, tourism was heralded as the "road to prosperity" even though the sector was vulnerable to the vagaries of world markets and the international political economy. As the industry was geared towards the affluent North American and, to a lesser degree, European societies, it was able to compete only by maintaining high standards of accommodation and hospitality. This required high levels of imports, especially food, and brought about inflated import bills and significant profit repatriation. By and large, tourism became an "enclave" within the Caribbean economy having few forward and backward linkages with, and contributing little to the development of other local sectors and activities and sustained growth (Payne and Sutton 2001: 4).

As these weaknesses of the modernization view were being exposed and debated by the region's governments and advisers,[3] radical scholars emphasized the dependence of the Caribbean economy on hegemonic centers for: markets and supplies, transfers of income and capital, banking and financial services, business and technical skills, and even for knowledge and ideas about themselves. While part of the broader international radical political economy analysis where development and underdevelopment were two sides of a single world capitalist system, and where underdevelopment followed, more or less, consequentially from dependency relationships between core and periphery, Caribbean dependency thought had its own special characteristics, associated with "the theory of plantation economy and society."

During the second phase, the early postcolonial period of the 1960s and 1970s, these notions grew into a distinct school of thought: the "Caribbean dependency thought." Dependency thinking generated intense scholarly and political debate, and had a significant impact on the intellectual and political life of the region and on government policies. It attributed the problems of development to the region's continuing epistemic, economic, cultural, and psychological dependence on the metropolitan world, and called for an extension of political decolonization to these spheres. The bulk of the explanation had come from systematic examination of the instruments that control the Caribbean economies, which brought about a lack of capacity to manipulate the operative mechanisms of the economic system along with several underdevelopment biases of plantation agriculture (Girvan 2006: 330; see also Table 2.1).

All these perspectives collectively constituted a powerful radical line of argument against the multifaceted conditions of dependency of the Commonwealth Caribbean, and undermined the intellectual credibility of the conventional modernization strategy that was pursued by Caribbean governments.[4] Indeed, the strong dismissal of the "industrialization by

Table 2.1 Overview of authors and themes in Caribbean dependency writings: 1960s and 1970s

Precursor	Core	Related
LEWIS	BEST	BREWSTER
Dual Economy	Epistemological Dependence	Interindustry Relations
Unemployment		Policy Dependence
Industrialization	BEST & LEVITT	
	Plantation Economy: Pure, Modified, Further Modified	BREWSTER & THOMAS
	New Mercantilism	Regional Economic Integration
		McINTYRE
	BECKFORD	Functional Dependence
	Plantation Economy	Trade Policy
	Plantation Society	Regional Economic Integration
	Psychological Dependence	
		DEMAS
	GIRVAN	Size and Dependence
	Mineral Export Economy	Regional Economic Integration
	Multinational Corporations	
		JEFFERSON
	THOMAS	Dependent Development
	Dependent Monetary Economy	
	Dependence and Transformation	ODLE
		Fiscal Dependence
		GIRVAN, ODLE, ARTHUR
		Technological Dependence

Source: Girvan 1996: 331 (Figure 1)

invitation" proposal as an "externally propelled" development strategy is a notable rejection of Lewis policy prescription. However, no strong alternative model of development and no thorough strategies were offered, and this serious shortcoming became the beginning of an impasse in the Caribbean development debate. Evidently, real-world experiments based on the prescriptive content of Caribbean dependency thought were often undermined by poor implementation, and had generally failed to promote self-reliant growth and political survival (Girvan 2006: 344). In addition, the collapse of the Grenadian revolution brought to an end the second phase of Caribbean development efforts.

In the 1980s, the third broad phase in Caribbean development, the international climate had radically changed. The United States managed to reshape the agenda of politics and international political economy and was able to lay down the parameters of what could be done and even what could be articulated. In addition, the neoliberal policy prescription was enforced by the IMF and the World Bank under the "structural adjustment" programs. This policy package was guided by the mantra stabilize, privatize, and liberalize. Specific measures included, among other policies: trade reform marked by lower tariffs to open the economy to greater competition and efficiency; tax reform to remove distortions that retard the flow of investment into productive activity; and financial liberalization and privatization of state enterprises to improve their efficiency of operations and services. The main goal of neoliberalism with respect to economic development was to create in the region a growing number of market-based economies capable of competing successfully in international export markets.

However, the international recession of the early 1980s severely reduced demand for a number of the region's main exports, especially, bauxite, petroleum products and sugar, and reduced the number of tourists visiting Caribbean islands. "The paradox is that the *actual* dependence of Caribbean economies became more acute in the era of structural adjustment and globalization of the 1980s and 1990s. Heightened indebtedness and the dismantling of traditional trade preferences have increased the economic vulnerability of Caribbean countries, exposing them to pervasive external intrusions into domestic policy making in the form of conditionalities imposed by the Washington-based international financial institutions and bilateral donors" (Girvan 2006: 345). What was seen was three crises in one in nearly all Caribbean economies: balance of payments constraints, fiscal imbalances, and a national debt crisis. Besides, the market-based reforms did not deliver the expected economic growth and employment levels. Desperate for financial support, Commonwealth Caribbean nations turned to the IMF and other multilateral financial institutions. As a result, their governments were forced to follow the neoliberal prescription during the 1980s and beyond. The favored policy measures were the same: liberalization of foreign exchange and import controls, devaluation of the currency, and the deflation of domestic demand. After following this prescription, the economy in question would be ready to return to the global marketplace able to achieve higher levels of exports and economic growth.

What is most striking about the Caribbean's embrace of neoliberalism in the 1980s is that the intellectual driving force behind its development strategy came, once again, from outside the region. However, the social costs of such neoliberal policies, measured in terms of unemployment, inflation, growing poverty and sharply declining living standards, were immense. At the end of the 1980s, Caribbean economies still faced major structural problems associated with the character of their production base and the distribution of their economic assets. Critical analyses of the economic and social impact of structural adjustment appeared and had their impact, especially in drawing attention to the peculiarly harsh costs imposed by such programs (Polanyi-Levitt 1991, among others). In addition, neoliberal prescriptions failed miserably to chart any sort of realistic alternative course of action for Caribbean governments in the critical arenas of economic management and national development.[5]

The last phase of Caribbean development efforts, the 1990s and beyond, was characterized by what might be called the consolidation of the neoliberal revolution, tempered only by the realization that more policy attention had to be paid to human resource development if the new technological imperatives of a globalizing economy were not to pass the region by. The agreement establishing the World Trade Organization in 1994, in which all Caribbean countries participate, "extends international trade disciplines to services, intellectual property, and the treatment of [transnational] corporations, thereby significantly constricting the policy space previously available to developing countries. National development of the kind that was the accepted objective in the era of decolonization has been replaced by the mantra of integration into the global economy. The new dependency associated with globalization is presented as *inter*dependence in the effort to obfuscate its asymmetries" (Girvan 2006: 345). Development was seen as a market-driven private sector-led process. The role of the state should be to meet the demands for "good governance" based on efficiency considerations and imposed by the international financial institutions, thereby fashioned to submissively serve the logic of deregulated competitive markets and integrated global production, led and directed by powerful transnational corporations.

Indeed, under the influence of the neoliberal narrative, the belief that emerged throughout the developing world by the 1990s, including the Caribbean, was that national economic growth could be significantly enhanced via links with major international economic actors such as multinational corporations, by encouraging foreign direct investment and privatization projects. In this undertaking, the role of the state was essential in facilitating the process for greater economic integration and for securing the emergence of a socio-economic order in which the market itself functioned as a form of social regulation—the ultimate goal of the neoliberal vision.

Key Aspects of an Alternative Development Paradigm for the Caribbean

If we were to consider the present state of orthodox and "New Right" economics, we would find that there has been little of worth contributed to framing rational strategies to cope with those complex problems which center on developing the productive forces of the small, open, dependent and underdeveloped economies of the Caribbean. In these analyses, geographical determinism seeks to explain underdevelopment as a product of the limitations of the physical environment (in terms of soil, natural resources and climate), while cultural notions may also be taken into consideration. Consequently, little attention has been paid to developing thorough planning frameworks to deal with the multidimensional problems of underdevelopment and material exploitation in the specific context of the small dependent economies of the Caribbean region. More specifically, neoclassical and neoliberal theories of growth, characterized by a vexing absence of historical understanding and awareness (i.e., the poverty of orthodox analysis), do not place emphasis on designing development strategies for transforming small dependent economies, which must undergo this transformation during the present neocolonial era (Thomas 1974).

Nevertheless, "smallness" is not the cause, but the spatial, demographic, and resource context in which socio-political relations are formed and developed, and the mode of production is organized. In other words, smallness can be simply interpreted as constituting, in a certain sense, an additional aspect of underdevelopment: of the nature of the structural dependence of small underdeveloped economies on international capitalism. As a consequence, the strength of indigenous political, social, cultural and economic forces and institutions *vis-à-vis* international capitalism is vastly inferior. Besides, the conjunction of production relations and productive forces in the region is of such a character and is organized in such a way that Caribbean communities have internalized through their social relations of production and the use of their productive forces a pattern of consumption that does not represent the needs of the community, and a pattern of production that is not oriented to either local consumption or domestic needs (Thomas 1974: 58–59). In fact, international trade and capital flows can penetrate deeper into the workings of the dependent small island economies of the Caribbean, affecting their production structures in general, and income distribution, job creation, and productivity growth in particular. Therefore, the notion of smallness has to be seen within a "holistic development" perspective which allows for dynamic changes in population, resources, output, technology, competency and institutions.

Also, most Caribbean countries' output and exports rely heavily on one or two industries (e.g., tourism in the services sector, energy-related products in the manufacturing sector, and bananas or sugar in the agricultural sector). But despite the relatively high *per capita* incomes for a number of Caribbean countries, many have substantial social development problems, such as high poverty rates, income inequality, unemployment, underemployment, and susceptibility to external forces (including weather, U.S. economic fluctuations, and changes in global commodity prices).

Between the early 1960s and the early 1980s, the majority of Britain's Caribbean colonies gained independence, and even though the colonial power had formally departed, it left in place political institutions and norms based on Britain's Westminster model of government. However, while the state has survived as a democratic institution (largely so), it lost a great deal of its effectiveness as a development tool because it was transformed into a mechanism for winning elections and meeting populist demands. Because of the "winner takes all syndrome" in Caribbean territories, the state became an instrument of disintegration rather than an institution around which society could cohere to deal with the development challenges. In a small society, the state is a large institution as an employer and dispenser of resources—hence the intense desire by various groups, not just special interests, to capture it. Still, fiscal budgets in the Caribbean *via* the political process often reflect the view of the political parties in power, and the class and interest group biases are usually maintained. In fact, although this deliberate policy is used, the politicization of the budgetary process in Caribbean states highlights programs and policies which are akin to what is called "pork barrel policies." This process has a great deal of importance in shaping fiscal policies of Caribbean states.

Since the 2000s, orthodox development policy proposals by international organizations (U.S. International Trade Commission 2008; UN-ECLAC 2012; IMF 2013)[6] and local economists have been offered as *modern* economic solutions to the region's complex problems. However, these orthodox policy recommendations—which by and large focus on total factor productivity, market-conforming suggestions, and more effective governance—have not resulted in significant socio-economic development, local industrial growth, endogenous competency and competitiveness. While conducive macroeconomic policies can contribute much towards enhancing the performance of Caribbean economies, such policies can only deal with the "symptoms" of economic problems. Arguably, the general concept of a developmental role for the state is rather alien to the general economic and political culture in the Caribbean.

However, in contrast to state interventions which are consonant with the *market failure* analysis, a government attempting to actively boost industrial growth needs to have a dominant developmental orientation. For these reasons, and perhaps for others, the construction of a production-based approach to economic development and a much sharper focus on strategic industrial policy should be important parts of a "Caribbean-type" developmental state framework—even though the lessons to be drawn from the success of the East Asian experience are themselves very controversial, are seen to be necessary to resolve structural problems, and offer concrete alternative solutions to Caribbean economies. Indeed, strategic industrial policy targets and centers around key strategic sectors, which can be expected to fuel diversification, industrial renaissance, and self-sustained economic growth. By recognizing differentiation of new and promising activities, particular branches and industrial sectors, thorough technically proficient policy can take care of the necessary human, material, and financial requisites and thus become effective (Karagiannis 2002). But a thorough identification of strategic targets depends on the democratic specification of multiple political goals, especially in view of possible trade-offs between different goals, and on the capability of the administration to pick or create the potential "winners" with reference to these goals.

Which industries will be able to respond to national interests in the future is a crucial question of industrial targeting. The main objective of such an important undertaking must be to increase rigor and effectiveness in the selection of strategic industries, promoting a more transparent procedure of decision making. This objective builds on the idea to clearly identify a rigorous priorities formation and to modify or fix certain criteria useful in supporting the identification of strategic industries, given the selected national and regional goals. This justifies why industrial targeting as an essential component of a national development agenda requires clear and transparent specification of political priorities and rationales that aim to be more certain, more transparent, and more immune to social and political pressures, partial interests, and policy makers' discretionality.

In some sectors, the region already has a strong basis on which to build (tourism and hospitality, entertainment, agro-processing, and food production). These sectors as well as modern activities of high potential—like those based on alternative or renewable forms of energy—require significant investment, rejuvenation and repositioning, and have to address a number of serious economic, social, institutional, and environmental issues simultaneously. Provided that the immediate problems are solved, the targeted sectors are clearly capable of considerable further expansion. In fact, the mutually beneficial relationship between different types of tourism and planned industrial activities of high growth potential and achievability can provide the solid foundation on which alternative endogenous development strategies can build. Once the priorities are right, and with effective "policy spillovers," resources will increasingly be allocated efficiently, production, productivity and profitability will increase, and the propulsive and dynamic sectors will become increasingly attractive to the private sector.

In addition, the approach used here seeks to link the process of growth and change in various sectors with that in the economy as a whole. On the other hand, the growth process in conjunction with higher levels of tourist arrivals are expected to lead to a widening of local markets, which in turn can bring about better transportation and communications systems. After resources have been developed and/or put to use, better industrial capabilities will broaden the Caribbean production base, will anchor the growth of domestic knowledge and technological capacity, and will provide sufficient stimulus to the mobilization of resources of all kinds and the inducement to invest. But domestic industrial capabilities formation (which encompasses knowledge, financial, and technical supporting institutions) is a sequential and cumulative process that can flourish in an environment of macroeconomic and political stability.

There is no need for vast bureaucratic machinery and procedure because the approach is clearly entrepreneurial. Such a radical approach needs to: emphasize substantive national development goals while being mindful of the constraints that the international political economy imposes; consider key relevant aspects of the East Asian trajectory towards boosting production expansion while making the necessary modifications to reflect the Caribbean history, culture, social psychology and politico-institutional arrangements; acknowledge the importance of authoritative and focused government agencies in overseeing the course of Caribbean industrial resurrection; and determine the quality and impact of policy intervention. A successful implementation, however, will require wide consultation, broad consensus, government intervention of high quality, determination, realism, commitment, and special emphasis on production-oriented growth.

The proposed framework takes into account dynamic relations among a number of "stylized facts": local resources, capital, social structure, technology and skills, scale and scope, institutions, history, culture, and social psychology. Such a pragmatic policy approach can successfully contribute to long-term supply-side initiatives aimed at creating or promoting selected sectors and prioritized activities, and can create economies of scale and scope, conditions and opportunities conducive to faster growth of existing and incoming enterprises (a "big push"). Economies of scale and learning will bring about multiple effects on, and changes in, the structure of local economies. The objective, of course, would be to improve industrial capabilities, increase both value add to the sectors and job opportunities, and strengthen forward and backward linkages, which would then be capable of spilling their expansionary forces into other sectors and activities: the support and development of indigenous resources, firms, and industries; the maximum utilization of investment (mainly in relevant R&D, innovation and skills to support new distinctively Caribbean industries); the removal of constraints on both the demand and supply sides which are imposed by the narrow size of the local markets and poor manufacturing base of Caribbean nations; an improvement in the range of services available to people and to industry (e.g., transportation, information, communication); the exploitation of economies of scale and scope; the application of productivity-enhancing production methods and techniques so as to raise industrial performance and competitiveness; the rejuvenation, restructuring, diversification, and global repositioning of Caribbean economic activity; and, the capacity to correct the Caribbean tendency toward external disequilibrium and high dependency on foreign economic activity, and withstand the effects of future cyclical downswings and structural changes (Karagiannis 2002).

Specifically, the following sets of policy and reforms are deemed to be necessary:[7]

1. Aggregate demand—along "functional finance" lines—and aggregate supply interaction

2. Egalitarian socially-sensitive policies (as important causal components of economic growth) to address real, basic needs of large population segments of Caribbean societies

3. The need for national strategic planning systems in place (FDIs would have to be positioned within such planning frameworks)

4. Thorough, technically proficient industrial growth strategies

5. Mixture of domestic and competitive developmentalism (with a more inward focus in the first instance and export promotion coming as an extension)

6. Selective incentives, disincentives, and planned investments on the modern factors of local growth and competency

7. Greater emphasis on production and operations quality

8. Enabling political, economic, and other social institutions; necessary politico-institutional reforms and enhanced democratic participation.

Culturally, the idea of underdevelopment can be seen as a "mental structure" (to paraphrase Wolfgang Sachs), where the underdeveloped nations desire to be like the developed ones. However, the Western lifestyle may neither be a realistic nor a desirable goal for the Caribbean population, as "externally endorsed" development can exacerbate underdevelopment and may result in a loss of a country's culture, people's perception of themselves, and modes of life. Uncritical borrowing of foreign models without the intervening stage of endogenous theoretical formulation serves merely to import ideas which neither recognize the possibilities of change permitted by local conditions nor respect the limits on these possibilities imposed by them.[8] Clearly, dependency thinking has been an important part of the oppositional tradition in the sphere of knowledge, and one of various manifestations of resistance in the behavioral, religious, ideological and philosophical elements that have their roots deep within Caribbean society, with its experience of colonialism, slavery, and indentured servitude (New World Group 1971: 241; Girvan 2006: 347).

Furthermore, notions like "poverty" are very culturally embedded and can differ a lot among cultures. Recent years have seen a spate of interest in holistic development aspects due to disenchantment with the complacent orthodoxy and failed neoliberalism. As the institutes which voice concern over underdevelopment are very Western-oriented, genuine, distinctively Caribbean national development efforts call for a broader cultural involvement in development thinking, and propose a vision of society which removes itself from the ideas and social psychology which currently dominate it. Ultimately, the best road ahead can only be found by way of analysis of history, and of the specific economic, social, and cultural conditions of the society (New World Group 1971: 241). Such a holistic development approach for Caribbean territories is interested instead in local culture and knowledge, a critical view against established sciences, and the promotion of local grassroots movements. In addition, social change is absolutely vital in order to reach solidarity, reciprocity, and a larger involvement in local knowledge enhancement.

Needless to say, any hope for a shift in economic and social policy away from the neoliberal project mandates the radicalization of popular struggles. Dependency thought resonates with other currents of critical and counter-hegemonic perspectives in the Caribbean and in the global South (Girvan 2006: 347). Challenging neoliberalism at the intellectual and ideological level alone is hardly sufficient for compelling policymakers to confront the deadly shortcomings of the dominant socio-economic policies and embark in turn on development strategies that help improve the overall conditions of Caribbean societies. What is required within each particular nation is the spread of a social movement that believes in an alternative future but relies on its own national experience to overcome underdevelopment, economic pressures and social injustice while building bridges of international solidarity with other like-minded movements and governments.

Challenging neoliberal globalization does not imply a rejection of globalization itself but reflects a wider global project of counter-hegemonic resistance which calls into question the nature of economic, social, and cultural interconnectedness that define the contemporary world. Social movements and activists bent on weakening or even overthrowing neoliberal policies in their respective territories should study the contemporary history of anti-globalization struggles for useful insights and appropriate strategies.[9] As recent experience in several Latin American, Asian, and

European countries has demonstrated, an alternative future to "barbaric neoliberalism" is very much possible.

Concluding Remarks

The chapter has sought to describe the historic impact of colonialism on the Caribbean development; present Caribbean development efforts since the end of World War II; carefully make the case for centralized political involvement in industrial expansion in the era of neoliberal globalization; and propose essential themes and notions towards framing an alternative egalitarian development paradigm for the region.

In the past, critical thought has identified the way in which the Caribbean was integrated into the world economy as principal explanation for the region's poverty and underdevelopment. The modern challenge is to "monitor and assess the impact of constant changes in the international economy on the region's development possibilities." On this basis, critical thought must fashion new strategies for "active participation in the world economy on terms which are favorable to the region's economies and peoples" (Witter and Lindsay 1996: xxvi).

Evidently, the recent globalization era has already impacted the economies and societies of the Caribbean. As the effects of globalization will more likely intensify, and given its complexity and its potentially disruptive power along with its opportunities, there is clearly an urgent need to understand it, to take advantage of whatever benefits it offers, and to minimize potentially negative outcomes. However, to successfully confront contemporary realities, institutional policy intervention ought to be a crucial positive force in pursuing national purpose priorities.

Finally, an alternative holistic development paradigm for the Caribbean, influenced by the developmental state analysis, is proposed here. This developmental state argument is advanced as a necessary approach for the support of selected growth industries in the region while leaving space for stimulating further social and political development. Mindful of both its limitations and the need for the relevant and necessary modifications, this approach tries to develop through rigorous planning societies that are prepared to go to the next level of development. For a realistic understanding of a development process, one has to take seriously into account history, culture, geopolitics, and modern international relations, and firmly base discussion on the evolution and interconnectedness of the national and global socioeconomic settings in which Caribbean economies and societies operate.

Notes

1. Lewis, W. A. (1950). "The Industrialization of the British West Indies", *Caribbean Economic Review* 2(1): 1–51; and (1954). "Economic Development with Unlimited Supplies of Labour", *Manchester School* 22(2): 139–191.
2. See UN-ECLAC, various national accounts and economic statistics during the last 50 years or so; Caribbean Development Bank (CDB), *Social and Economic Indicators*, various issues; and CARICOM Secretariat (2013), *CARICOM's Selected Economic Indicators 2002–2011*. www.caricomstats.org
3. Overall, as the Commonwealth Caribbean Regional Secretariat admitted in 1972 (*From CARIFTA to Caribbean Community*. Georgetown):

   [The postwar era of growth represented] a continuation of the centuries-old pattern of West Indian economy—growth without development; growth accompanied by imbalances and distortions; growth generated from outside rather than within; growth without the fullest possible use of West Indian manpower, entrepreneurial, capital and natural resources; growth resting on a foreign rather than indigenous technological base; and growth accompanied by imported consumption patterns.

4. For a full discussion, see: Payne, A. and P. Sutton (2001). *Charting Caribbean Development*. London: Macmillan-Caribbean.
5. *Ibid*. See also Girvan, N. (2006). "Caribbean Dependency Thought Revisited", *Canadian Journal of Development Studies* 27(3): 329–352; Girvan, N. and O. Jefferson (eds) (1971). *Readings in the Political Economy of the Caribbean*. Mona, Jamaica: New World Group.
6. U.S. International Trade Commission (2008). *Caribbean Region: Review of Economic Growth and Development*; UN-ECLAC (2012). *Development Paths in the Caribbean*; IMF (2013). *Caribbean Small States: Challenges of High Debt and Low Growth*.
7. Karagiannis (2000–2013) has published extensively on these development policy issues. See, for example, Karagiannis, N. (2002). *Developmental Policy and the State: The European Union, East Asia, and the Caribbean*. Lanham, MD: Lexington Books. See also Thomas, C. Y. (1988). *The Poor and the Powerless: Economic Policy and Change in the Caribbean*. London: Latin American Bureau.

8. Another term used to describe this condition was "dysfunctional ideologizing" (Best 1965). See also Witter, M. and L. Lindsay (1996). "Introduction", in K. Polanyi Levitt and M. Witter (eds), *The Critical Tradition of Caribbean Political Economy: The Legacy of George Beckford*. Kingston, Jamaica: Ian Randle Publishers, xxi-xxvi.

9. A comparative analysis of anti-globalization strategies can be found in Amory Starr (2001). *Naming the Enemy: Anti-Corporate Movements Confront Globalization. London: Zed Books.*

CHAPTER 3

Public Sector Capacity for Governance in the Caribbean

Indianna D. Minto-Coy and Evan M. Berman

Summary

Chapter 3 defines and provides a general framework for governance capacity, looks at historical challenges of governance capacity in the Caribbean suggesting some patterns, and assesses the past performance of the public sector in the Caribbean context. Taking into consideration vexing challenges, modern demands, and expectations associated with the Region's developing states, the authors specify key areas for improving and strengthening their capacity for governance.

Introduction

Governance has become a fashionable term by which to describe the ability of countries and organizations to make decisions and address important challenges in effective ways. Economic development, public safety, social development, environmental sustainability, health, and education all require important policy choices. Caribbean countries face many challenges, indeed, and a long-standing concern is whether government jurisdictions in the Caribbean have adequate governance capacity, that is, whether they are up to the task of addressing challenges in the above and other areas. By example, while progress has been made in disaster responsiveness, it is clear that much more needs to be done in areas of prevention, transnational cooperation and resourcing. The same might be said of health care and economic development, too. It makes little sense to discuss sensible policies and reforms that countries are unable to adopt or implement in effective ways.

This chapter looks at the capacity for governance in the Caribbean. The first section defines and provides a general framework for governance capacity. The second section looks at historical challenges of governance capacity in the Caribbean suggesting some patterns. The third section examines some modern day issues around both policy and administration, allowing for conclusions about continuity and new issues in governance capacity. The empirical basis for the chapter rests in the many case studies presented in Minto-Coy and Berman (2016), and other studies. Along the way, we point to some successes in increasing governance capacity, as well. The latter is important given Grindle's point on good enough governance as pointing not only to shortfalls but also understanding what is working (2004).

The term "governance" is of recent vintage and quite abstract. The term became fashionable in the 1990s, notably among economists, interested in studying how rules, authority, norms and decision-making processes affect institutions/organizations as they address market and nonmarket (e.g., common) issues. The World Bank Report on *Governance and Development* (1992) also contributed significant attention to the emergence and popularity of the term in the developing context. Definitions of governance vary, with some authors defining it broadly as "processes of social organization and coordination" (Bevir 2012), allowing for broad, theoretical inquiry, and others studying specific arenas such as public governance, corporate governance, global governance or internet governance, and environmental governance. Fukuyama (2013), for example, addresses the public sector and defines governance as "a government's ability to make and enforce rules, and to deliver services." A key point for all authors is that 'governance' draws a distinction with 'government' in so far as issues involve multiple actors and, hence, a need for vertical and horizontal coordination (Hufty 2011). Also, while national and provincial governments continue to play important roles, issues are increasingly able to draw on increasingly capable private organizations and lower tier governments (cities, public authorities), hence, making it a timely concept. Governance also brings economists closer to disciplines such as public administration which studies authority, norms, and decision making.

Associated with governance is the normative term 'good governance' which, according to the World Bank (1994) is epitomized "by predictable, open and enlightened policy making; a bureaucracy imbued with a professional ethos; an executive arm of government accountable for its actions; and a strong civil society participating in public affairs; and all behaving under the rule of law." Other definitions also include good or equitable outcomes, and the UNDP (1997) notes that: "Good governance is, among other things, participatory, transparent and accountable. . . . and political, social and economic priorities are based on broad consensus in society and that the voices of the poorest and the most vulnerable are heard in decision making over the allocation of development resources." The Worldwide Governance Indicators (WGI) project aims to measure good governance that uses six dimensions: voice and accountability, political stability and absence of violence, government effectiveness, regulatory quality, rule of law, and control of corruption (World Bank 2015). While some critics suggest limits to the applicability of these "Western" notions (Bruhn 2009), concepts of integrity, equitability, and effectiveness have very broad appeal.

In short, governance has been an intellectual growth area during the past twenty years and is now part of accepted norm in academic and practice-based discourse. Studies in economics, public administration, public policy have increased awareness among policy makers that both "institutions matter" and "leadership matters," as is now reflected in emphases on integrity, strategic leadership, inclusiveness, and organizational effectiveness, as well as increased attention to policy outcomes in areas of inequality, social capacity, and problems of the commons (e.g., environment). In short, the capacity to get things done affects what gets done.

Framework for Capacity

Governance capacity is generally defined or discussed as having conditions and a set of capabilities that are needed for effective governance. While the term "governance capacity" has come into use, it is not well defined and often varies based on subject matter, similar to the term "governance" itself (e.g., environmental governance). In the context of public sector in Caribbean island nations, we define governance capacity as having conditions for planning, decision making, and execution of policies and programs that in both process and outcome are adequate with regard to effectiveness and being equitable.

This definition draws attention to necessary elements of governance, as well as necessary criteria for their assessment. As to the latter, Grindle (2004, 2007) draws attention to "good governance" setting unrealistically high standards, and the need for "good enough" governance that provide sufficient conditions for programs to be effective, such as poverty alleviation which is her focus. Here, we distinguish between 'good enough' (say, adequate) public sector governance capacity which concern rather minimal capabilities that allows small island nations to achieve adequate outcomes in light of their current challenges, and greater (say, superior) governance capacity that may allow for even better outcomes. The task is to think about good enough governance capacity, before moving on to even higher levels of capacity that may be unrealistic or unattainable at present. As is colloquially said, "the best is the enemy of the good" (enough).

While scholarship on public sector capacity is sparse, studies are plentiful on government and public sector effectiveness. Based on the latter, borrowing on public administration, other disciplines and notions of good (enough) governance, we provide the following framework for the governance capacity of nations (we call these as such, even though some Caribbean islands are dependent territories, of course):

A. Strategic Leadership that Serves All Population Groups

Nations must be able to make decisions that address their challenges. Public sector governance is distinguished by the need to make decisions that address both short- and longer-term time horizons, and which serve diverse populations (e.g., by income). In practice, these features are compromised by politics, forms of government and self-serving behavior of elite groups. First, many thousands of decisions are required, touching upon many different areas (public safety, health and education, labor and environmental regulation, economic development, etc.) and it is axiomatic that not all strategic decisions can come from political actors alone; senior bureaucrats must provide leadership, as well. Democracy is prone to legislative gridlock (e.g., U.S. Congress) and thus presidential orders and bureaucratic rule making are needed as forms of leadership, too. Good enough strategic leadership that means decisions and programs are developed for a nation's key issues and also that all programs receive periodic strategic reviews and updates; cooperation is needed among bureaucratic and political leaders on these matters.

Second, leadership elites in politics and/or bureaucracies are prone to becoming self-serving and insufficiently advancing minority or poor groups or the public interest. While Colonial powers are typically insufficiently concerned with these matters as priorities, their extractive goals, national or indigenous elites are not necessarily better when they, too, are self-serving and lack resources; examples from African nations are clear. The capacity of decision making also requires the ability of elites to regulate their own interests in favor of public and minority interests and have capacity for making decisions with mid- and long-term horizons. Good enough strategic leadership means sufficiently advancing the public interest and a nation's poor and minority populations. Good enough governance also requires decisions that are made in consultation and cooperation from other actors, including working with other nations and pursuing regional strategies where transnational issues and those of scope/scale require so. These are important features of governance capacity.

B. Resourcing

Governance requires money, and lots of it. Therefore, nations must be able to raise revenues in ways that requires taxation and reasonable borrowing practices. This requires tax collection, sound financial management, addressing tax avoidance, utilization of grants and international donor programs, and also economic management to ensure a future base. Insufficient resourcing will cause nations to be unable to pursue progress towards their key priorities; good enough reoccurring means that these key challenges can be met. It may also include ensuring that taxation burdens are perceived as being fairly distributed to further related purposes of social development and national cohesion.

C. Capable Bureaucracy

Public bureaucracies must have the ability to achieve policy aims in effective, efficient and fair ways. This is not necessarily about using the latest technology and management fad, but rather about being not wasteful and reliably effective in securing achievement "wins." Neither is it necessarily about size; the examples of Singapore, Hong Kong, New Zealand and Luxemburg all show that small states can be effective with small bureaucracies that are strategically focused and managed around highly capable civil servants providing superior performance. This is often achieved through rigorous and competitive selection, strong individual performance management, and the use of board and authorities that are run as much as possible on a business-like basis without undue personnel protections. It is also based on holding senior officials, appointed or not, accountable for the performance of their units.

Clearly, this is not always the practice in the Caribbean and elsewhere. At the other extreme are poorly managed public agencies that defer strategic decision making (perhaps to political institutions), lack technology and intelligence (data), appointees who are self-serving and lacking in commitment, and employees who lack motivation and compensation, and performance systems that are outdated and ineffective for the tasks. At issue here is defining "good enough" bureaucratic capability that ensures reasonably effective service. We think this may involve agencies that use performance strategies and technology that gets the job done, which are free of modest corruption (below), and having middle and senior managers who are amply imbued with public service ethos that make decisions which further public service with short- and long-term goals in mind. In today's governance, they should have capacity and desire for cooperation with other jurisdictions and private organizations and also work with other nations on transnational issues. It should be noted that another societal contribution of public sector bureaucracies is that they are routes to advancement for minorities and women due to their relatively stable employment.

D. Accountability

Governance involves the exercise of authority and, as two sayings go, "mistakes happen" and "power corrupts." Accountability (or rather, oversight) is needed to identify poor performance and abuse of power and ensure corrective actions for both. In short, nations need effective accountability processes and ensure that these processes or institutions have adequate independence and authority to do their job well. In this regard, a main critique is that some accountability institutions are de facto 'toothless tigers' or have become captured (corrupted) by those agencies or interests they are to oversee. Good enough accountability requires at least some capability for addressing the worst of abuses and for undertaking corrective action and ensuring minimal levels of acceptable performance from political and bureaucratic actors. Developing such systems has become among the challenging issues for democracies and one-party systems alike.

Anti-corruption emerged in recent years as a key priority in global agendas. Corruption is defined as the abuse of power or position to acquire a personal benefit or advantage. Public sector corruption includes corruption of the political process and of government agencies, not only affecting the allocation of public funds for contracts, grants, and hiring, but also strategic decision making, attention to public and minority needs, reducing tax compliance and burdens, increasing the cost of frontline services through petty bribes, advantages procured through revolving doors and more, in short, all of the above governance capacities. The opportunity for corruption and advantage exists at all levels—senior, middle, and lower levels, and nations with poor governance capacity often have a high incidence of corruption, as well. A critical governance capacity is having defined corruption broadly enough, and ensuring fair and effective anti-corruption investigation. It might be noted that Transparency International has done much to further awareness about corruption through its annual country reports, and also that e-government has done much in recent years to reduce corruption through accountability and transparency, which increases bureaucratic effectiveness and efficiency.

The above provides a framework for public sector governance capacity. No doubt, additional factors might be mentioned. Some of these might be viewed as *societal conditions* or even as preconditions that further public sector governance. Whether these are viewed as a fifth category (E) or as precondition is not a matter we wish to pursue here. One such factor is having adequate subnational governments and private sector organizations that can contribute to service delivery and problem-solving, hence reducing the demands on national governments. Another factor is sufficiently diversified and competitive private sector that supports economic growth and government resourcing. A third condition is having populations that are predisposed to demanding public ethos and leadership from their governments. A fourth factor is respect and abidance for the rule of law and democratic principles in the general populations; some populations and government actors appear to define themselves more by their extractive successes than their societal contributions. These and other societal conditions may affect governance capacity, as well. Though these factors are largely beyond the grasp of governance in the short-run, they should be the target of state sector policies and programs for increasing in the mid- to long-run. The overarching framework presented above also echoes Capano, Howlett and Ramesh's (2015) approach which takes in the policy and political aspects of governance capacity.

The Legacy of Governance Capacity in the Caribbean

Studies of the history of Caribbean island show a pattern of governance and governance capacity that have sometimes left a legacy which persists through the present. The harsh truth is that independence has not always brought good enough governance. This is not the place to review major histories of Caribbean islands, but rather to present analysis of them as regarding the above concepts.

Historical Overview of Governance Capacity in the Commonwealth Governance

Studies of the Commonwealth show that the organization of the public sectors in these countries was largely informed by the demands of the British and that economy (Minto-Coy 2016a; Wallace 1977). Whereas the region occupied a central place in British economy, focus was less on establishing stable societies beyond the dictates for stable plantation labor. As such, the organization was mainly top down, with emphasis on maintaining law and order. An efficient public service in this context was dictated by efficient cost-reduction to the Crown and for neat integration into the British Empire. Thus, whereas the region represented the frontier in which the British forged their global and economic dominance and as its importance waned with the abolition of slavery and the emancipation of the slaves, the value of the region also waned. In such a context the development of the local environment or policies geared to improving the livelihoods of the local population were not the main prerogative.

For sure, the organization of the public sector in the immediate post-independence years allowed for many of the brightest locals to enter the public service. Nonetheless, the top-down nature of the bureaucracy has been noted as having led to practices of exclusion in the practice of governance, a tendency towards secrecy around decisions and processes, risk-aversion and an unwillingness to break with norms and traditions. Indeed, where governance was preferences on the existence of a mass of population who lacked the experience, information or right mix of qualities to facilitate their engagement in the decision-making process then power and policy making becomes the task of a centralized and small group of elites. In such a context, the search for and implementation of better ways of governing in the independence years has not always been genuine, has been more ad hoc in contemplation and implementation. Attempts of reform have nonetheless, been hampered by poor planning and a failure to implement and evaluate. As such, opportunities for learning have been lost, a reality that has been compounded by the slow pace in moving towards evidence-based research.

Arguably one of the most defining features of the colonial legacy has been the Westminster Whitehall system of governance which purports the existence of an anonymous, neutral and impartial civil service tasked with the implementation of policies. In societies fraught with contentions over the distribution of scarce benefits and spoils, nepotism, clientelism, an early focus on years of service as opposed to merit for promotion, as in cases of ethnically-based grievances in places such as Guyana and Trinidad & Tobago, these goals have rarely been realized. Indeed, the sometimes combative relationship between political leaders and the bureaucracy has seen politics triumphing over bureaucracy and by extension sound advice and reason. To this end, appointments in the public sector sometimes take on a political undertone to the extent where it may be seen as reward for party political support as opposed to merit, with consequences for professionalism and actions in the public interest as opposed to those of the appointee.

This is an important consideration given the reality that the public interest is not to be taken naturally as being synonymous with the government's or Minister's interest. This is important with Ministers often more preoccupied with the rigors of the electoral cycle than in planning and staying the course of long-term development plans. Such is the case, for instance in the change of policies adopted by one political regime at the change of administration upon elevation. The desire not to be seen to be authenticating an opponent's policies has seen waste, duplication, implementation deficits, and problems in policy coordination even after money (including aid) has been exhausted on that project (Minto-Coy 2016a; Jones 1992). Indeed, even where civil servants have sought to adhere to the WW principles, they have not operated in environments in which such principles can thrive. So even without making normative judgements on the ability of such a civil servant to exist or whether good enough governance really calls for the existence of such characters, the reality is that these principles were not realized in the Caribbean then, neither can they be said to be pervading the same today. Indeed, perhaps an early realization of the challenges in meeting such ideals may have meant attention to engineering locally informed procedures for governance that would have in essence aimed at reducing the effects of some of the most pernicious features of government in the Commonwealth Caribbean.

One of the effects of public governance in such a context has been corruption. Indeed, it has been noted that corruption is largely an independence phenomenon (Mills 1997) while others have suggested its existence (as well as nepotism) during the colonial period and prior to independence. Perhaps the distinctive feature for the post-independence period is the extent of occurrence. That is, the incidence of corruption has increased as resources have become scarcer in economies that have not yet delivered the levels of growth and formal opportunities for enrichment envisioned prior to independence.[1]

Historical Overview of Governance Capacity in the French Antilles

One of the guiding themes in the public administration history of the French Caribbean[2] is the fact of an underdeveloped bureaucracy. A large contributing factor here has been the insertion of the region into the central administrative apparatus of the French government, to the extent that little power, participation, and ownership has been realized at the local level. There has been little opportunity for the contextualization of public governance, the development of internally informed management and leadership capacity. This practice has been embodied in the principles of assimilation, centralization, uniformity, and universalism which featured in the conferring of the status of overseas departments (*Departements d'outre mer*—DOM). As such, the organization of public governance was not based on local context with France maintaining close control over public policies, and the very social and economic organization of the Caribbean.

Insertion into the French administrative system has had significant implications including the stifling of local innovation and policy making capacity. Attempts to raise standard of living to the level of France has led to frustrated ambitions locally particularly where citizens in the Caribbean are not viewed as equal to those in France. Emphasis on cultural inclusion and raising living standards has not been matched by similar attention to assisting the islands to becoming internally sustainable and hence stronger, more economically independent units within the French empire. As such, the DOMs remain some of the most economically deprived in the EU and reliant on the mainland for their very survival.

Historical Overview of Governance Capacity in the Dutch Antilles

One of the evolving themes in the history of the Caribbean is the ongoing struggle to re-define its relationship with former colonial powers and the tensions inherent in such a struggle. In the case of the Dutch territories, the initial focus on Dutchinalizing the region saw the intentional introduction of a Dutch system of public governance in key areas such as the civil service and education. Under such a system the emphasis of the civil service was more on file keeping and little about the development of local economies. Indeed, this theme has followed most of the Dutch region throughout the transition to the different levels of association between the mainland and the territories over the years including independence (Suriname in 1975, and Aruba in 1986). The most recent transition in 2010 has seen the Netherlands Antilles transitioning to various levels of association with islands such as Curacao becoming autonomous partners and others (e.g., Saba) municipalities.

The different sentiments and associations as it relates to association with the Netherlands underlines a lack of collaboration and identification with each other and more towards the mainland. Indeed, throughout the wider Caribbean, the institutionalization of the cultural and governance institutions of the colonial powers has been the successful theme stymying meaningful partnering across islands with collaboration across historical colonial boundaries.

Key public posts as in the French Caribbean and colonial days of the Commonwealth region were occupied by civil servants directly coming from the mainland or light-skinned locals. Frustrated desires and exclusion in the colonial periods have evolved into corruption and inefficient public governance in more recent times of greater self-rule and independence. These developments have surfaced in the politicization of the civil service and its use as a tool for distributing political patronage and reward. The result has been an oversized public sector which is hierarchical and sometimes not fit for purpose (i.e., skills, training and organization). Tensions between the political and administrative machinery have also stymied efforts at developing the capacity and ability of the latter to deliver quality service with politicians shying away from granting too much power to their counterparts.

The economic (aid and loans) support from the mainland, as in the case of the French Caribbean has had the effect of stifling local economic growth and debt in still dependent territories. Additionally, periods of economic support did not entail the need to develop local economies. Furthermore, spending has not been tempered by the actual income but has continued as in periods where the Netherlands was fully responsible for the region. Efforts to temper high public debt and the conflated public service have seen more recent attempts to restrict spending and hiring in the public sector. The emerging concern now surrounds the aging of the public sector.

Governance Capacity in Other Caribbean Territories

Many of the experiences surrounding the development and demonstration of governance capacity above has played out in various forms in the remainder of the region. In the case of territories such as Cuba and Haiti, their particular histories have seen periods of isolation from their other Caribbean neighbors and the world. To this end, they have been denied support for the development of sound governance institutions. The impact in both cases has diverged significantly with important implications for governance capacity and experiences in these two countries.

Whereas Cuba was to receive some support from the former USSR, Cuba has devised local capacities and creative governance. Evidence is seen in the quality of the education and health systems, in indigenously derived science and technology (e.g., pharmaceuticals) and related social indicators that rival those of many developed countries. These achievements have been accomplished amidst a longstanding U.S. embargo that has since 2014 appeared to be nearing its end. Importantly, Haiti's exclusion arguably appeared to have been more complete and longstanding (given the extended period of Haiti's independence and the very way in which that country secured its independence) (Minto-Coy and Berman 2016). In Haiti's case, the result has been a failing economy, ongoing weaknesses in public sector capacity and organization as seen in informality, corruption, enduring poverty and the sustained failure of governments to organize or function effectively. To be sure, one defining features of governance has been the absence of a well-intentioned elite in Haiti and arguably, its presence in Cuba in so far as there was willingness to govern beyond self and family interests for a perceived wider good.

Collectively, the historical development of the Caribbean's public sector capacity therefore cannot be divorced from the legacies and emergence of the region as colonial outposts. The resulting impact on the capacity for public sector governance has been profound, ranging from the emergence of conflated and underdeveloped bureaucracies, financial mismanagement, corruption, absence of local concerns and context in the policy process, failure to effectively develop and manage human resources for development, to the development of rule and rote form of public governance that has reduced responsiveness and innovation. The public sector then, has not been seen enough as an active contributor and vital informant of the region's growth and developmental potential. For instance, swelling the ranks of the civil service without consideration of the impact on national budgets, corruption, and the use of the public sector as a tool for dispensing rewards and punishments has compromised the ability to hire the best and efficient capacity management, while the mismanagement of public finances has contributed to debt and high balance of payments resulting in sustained inability to finance development interventions. This approach is also seen in the inability of the state to marshal different actors (e.g., business and society) behind the developmental agenda (some exceptions being seen in Barbados) and even in the conflict which sometimes typifies the politico-bureaucratic relationship. The inability to link the quality of the public administration apparatus to the imperative of raising incomes and economic growth have seen a divorce of thinking on the place of the public sector in growth. The relationship with the colonial powers did not entail an emphasis on the development of local (financial, institutional, organizational or human) capacity for governance, less good governance. For the most part, the black population across the region were largely kept out of governance institutions and mechanisms. From a state of exclusion and external orientation and without direct intent otherwise it would be difficult to derive public capacity that was sympathetic to the local needs. It is perhaps for this reason that inequality remains such a prevalent feature of many Caribbean societies today.

Public Sector Capacity in Modern Times

Much of the current reality of governance in the Caribbean can be traced back to the enduring colonial legacies and transplanted governance systems across the region. As will be shown here, however, many capacity gaps also have their basis in the independence or modern experiences forming a complex interplay between old and new. Before this however, it is important to note that there have been areas of success and definite steps towards addressing capacity gaps in select areas including efforts at institution building via public sector reform and modernization in public financial management (PFM). This section discusses some of these improvements. We also draw general conclusions about public sector capacity for governance in the Caribbean in the twenty-first century.

A. Capacity Development in Tourism and Telecommunications Policy

One of the more successful areas is demonstrated in the achievements in the tourism industry with the Caribbean being one of the more successful globally. While the industry largely emerged without much planning, governments have recognized the need for specific policy interventions in growing, diversifying, and protecting what remains the largest contributor to Caribbean economies. As such more precise steps have included the development of infrastructure and policy framework governing the sector (Clayton, Karagiannis, and Bailey 2016).

Elsewhere too, some governments have demonstrated a desire to move away from archaic regulations and legislation by introducing new practices and using policy to open up opportunities for business and citizens. Evidence can be seen in the areas of telecommunications where governments in the English-speaking territories have succeeded in removing monopoly arrangements in the telecommunications industry, many of which were vestiges of colonial ties. In reforming the structure and conduct of the communications sector in the first decade of the twenty-first century, the region has taken decisive steps towards breaking the close ties between the monopoly incumbent and policymakers and regulators in the sector (Minto-Coy 2016b, 2009a), though the challenges of regulatory capture reoccur from time to time.

The introduction of innovative regulatory models including the adoption of a regional approach to telecommunications regulation (and banking) in the Organization of Eastern Caribbean States (OECS) has been noted for their innovativeness. The approach to a joint regulator (ECTEL) has been useful in addressing the shortage in regulatory expertise, while sharing the costs of sector regulation.

The steps being taken by policymakers in countries such as the Dominican Republic and Jamaica, have also seen some islands becoming important players in international discourse on emerging issues. Included here is the emerging open data and open data for development movements, the next evolution in the focus on e-government. These developments have been achieved through partnership with local research community and international allies demonstrating the benefits of cross-section and national partnerships. Early developments here act as indicators on how transformation in the regulations and structure of the telecommunications industry since the early 2000s can be extended to bring greater transparency, accountability and citizen engagement, as well as open opportunities for innovation and entrepreneurship.

B. Gains in PSR Reform & Public Financial Management

One of the lingering challenges in the region is the need for public sector reform (PSR) and the inability to manage public finances effectively. Individual territories such as the Cayman Islands have fared better than others, in its desire to maintain sound public financial management (PFM). As is clear from the previous section however, the issues around PSR and PFM affect the entire region and its ability to realize good enough governance.

To the Caribbean's credit there has been recognition of the need for improvements in these areas, with positive advances particularly in the aftermath of the Global Financial Crisis of 2008, towards achieving better financial governance. Measures include the move towards result-oriented budgeting, automation, and improvements in the legal framework around financial management. Emphasis has also been placed on debt restructuring and management, containing public spending and tax reform and administration. One of the main areas here is the need to contain spending overall but particularly on wages and pensions, a relevant issue given the role of governments as the main employer.

Deeply related to sound PFM is the issue of public sector reform. This is so given that the public sector is integrally involved in planning and executing national budgets and its size makes it a costly organ to finance. As it relates to public sector reform, much has been realized in raising the standard of public service in some countries, including among the UK-type executive agencies introduced in countries such as Belize, Jamaica, Guyana, and Trinidad & Tobago from the end of the 1990s (Minto-Coy 2016a & 2010; Bissessar 2002; Sutton 2008). Reforms include improvements in training, the introduction of performance management systems, and attempts at decentralization with public services once based in cities now being accessible in rural areas. Decentralization has been about extending access but also addressing another legacy issue, i.e., transforming the inherited hierarchical bureaucratic model to allow civil servants more ownership and voice in operations.

The experiences of Jamaica exemplify some of the perversions in public sector governance highlighted above, while the most recent reforms (post 2012) suggest the possibility for successful capacity enhancement. The former scenario has received much attention (including Minto-Coy 2011a; Harriott 2008; Blavy 2006; Sampson 1996; World Bank 2006; Gray 2004;

Jones 1992) but it is to the more recent and still evolving reforms that we turn briefly. Undertaken mainly since 2012 and under the support and funding of the IMF, the country has within a short term introduced a number of reforms in PSR and PFM that have already begun to reap visible benefits, including improvement on the World Economic Forum's Global Competitiveness ranking from 107 in 2011 to 86 in 2016 (Trading Economics 2016). Among these is the early and simultaneous tabling of the Estimates of Expenditure and Revenues in 2015 which marked the first time that these were tabled together in the history of independent Jamaica (Jamaica Observer 2015). Rather than agree to specific demands for wage increases which in the past would have occurred specifically in an election period, the government refrained from doing so. Instead, allowances and benefits were granted, for example, funeral benefits and the establishment of an education fund in the form of grants to the children of public sector workers (Linton 2015) helping to deliver more modest wage increases and adhering to the intent to contain budget shortfalls. Other reforms include the removal of discretionary waivers above certain levels helping to reduce the abuses that have tended to accompany the system of waivers in Jamaica. The implementation of the reform program has been carefully monitored by the Economic Program Oversight Committee specifically created for this purpose. Membership represents some of the most successful business leaders and public sector representatives with information being released by the committee to assist the public in monitoring the country's progress and achievements under the program. The country's tackling of corruption has also improved moving from number 86 (of 175 countries) in 2011 to 69 in 2015 based on the Transparency International's Corruption Perceptions Index. In essence, there has been a coming together of an understanding of the role of PSR and sound PFM to the growth and sustainable advancement of that country. The developments since 2012 suggest that Caribbean leaders do have the ability and where there is sufficient desire, can make major transformations for the benefit of their citizens across the region.

C. Emergency Management

While much of the discussion on capacity has tended to focus on man-made or legacy issues, no discussion of public sector capacity in the

Caribbean can go without mention of the impact of natural disasters as a major constraint on the ability of Caribbean governments to govern effectively. Its geographical location has made the Region prone to natural and climatic conditions whose impacts are far more pronounced due to small size and resources (Minto-Coy and Berman 2016: 21). The impact of hurricane Tomas on St Lucia in 2010 amounted to 43.4 percent of GDP (ibid).

The response, particularly of the English-speaking Caribbean demonstrates the inventiveness and ability to build resilience in the face of serious governance threats. Faced with this natural risk, the region has developed a sophisticated range of interventions to environmental and disaster risk management. Of note here is the evolution in programs and approach from a piecemeal one to focusing on all stages of a hazard including prevention and mitigation. The evolution in approaches and sustained capacity building is evidenced in the name change of the Caribbean Disaster Emergency Response Agency (CDERA) established in 1990 to Caribbean Disaster Emergency Management Agency (CDEMA) in 2009 (Granvorka et al. 2016). The evolution of the region's approach has been orchestrated at the national and regional levels with multisector involvement including international donors. Indeed, this has been one of the areas in which the Caribbean has made significant advancements, demonstrating some proclivity towards proactive action and strategic leadership which differs from the, lethargy or inertia which pervades other areas of governance.

D. Capacity in Education and Health

Education and health systems have evolved significantly moving from the elitism and preoccupation with the North which typified access and design under colonialism to ones based on inclusion and meeting the needs of local and regional populations. Of course, many gaps remain and are emerging in the provision of these services. This is likely to be so as governments face increasing challenges in meeting national budgets and islands such as Barbados reduced subventions to University students.

Nevertheless, the region has seen success in the development of human resources and the evolution in its educational system. Citizens are employable globally and regionally with the expansion in the number of training institutions and upgrading of facilities. The Region is not only a place for educating nationals but international students as well. This has been facilitated through the development of a number of schools (e.g., medical education in Grenada) targeting international students and attempts at internationalization (at the program level) at a number of other educational institutions across the region (e.g., the Mona School of Business and Management).

Expansion in provision has also been witnessed in the health sector. The focus has also evolved in response to recognized needs of the region at different phases of its evolution (Jules and Fryer 2016). Successes have come in addressing issues related to nutrition, water and sanitation. Nevertheless, capacity remains strained with increased challenges around funding and provision. Responses have included the introduction of user fees and a multisectoral and decentralized approach to planning and implementation. Indeed, while no region is arguably free of such challenges, new and emerging health risks associated with diseases such as chikungunya, Zika-virus have underscored capacity-gaps in terms of manpower, research capacity, technological and financial resources. HIV/AIDS-related deaths and infant mortality rates suggest further weaknesses in the health system. The tendency towards a regional response in the English-speaking region has also been compromised after the 2008 global financial crises with countries moving towards unilateral health sector governance. As new challenges emerge the health and education systems will continue to be tested further with sustained reliance on external sources for technical and financial support.

E. Lingering Issues in Caribbean Public Sector Capacity

The issues and themes raised in this section indicate advancement in governance capacity. Many of the areas discussed suggest success where efforts are made towards good enough governance or improvement within given constraints. The cases indicate that there is the ability to tackle pressing governance challenges across the region. Ultimately, the Caribbean has given rise to a variety of forms and quality of public governance with varying effects. The scattering of countries along the development spectrum (from Barbados to Haiti) underscores this point. Nevertheless, lingering concerns remain. As such, we draw some conclusions about capacity in the Caribbean.

In spite of the ongoing preoccupation with PSR, the ailments continue. Indeed, if successful PSR globally have in the main been comprehensive in their focus and support (Minto-Coy 2011b), it is clear that the experiences of improving public sector capacity in the Caribbean have faltered given misleading and conflicting messages, failure to coalesce vital support (from society and public servants themselves) around reform. Some of the challenges here can be attributed to ineffective leadership and communication skills among leaders who have not yet fully welcomed nonstate actors including, the private sector and citizens as attractive governance partners. This has been levelled at the neo-liberal New Public Management model of reform adopted since the 1990s that has seen the introduction of a number of reform concepts that have not taken route locally (Sutton 2008).

For example, performance appraisals and management and performance based remuneration have been difficult to realize in the public sector with appraisals being delayed or having little relationship with salaries or promotion. As noted by Bissessar, promotion is still based on seniority rather than performance (2002). Furthermore, poor performance has not been met with any adverse action, which goes further to demotivate those public servants who would wish to go beyond the base level of service.

Ultimately, this speaks to insufficient levels of accountability, which is also deeply rooted in the lack of ownership of results and reform movements (good and bad). This is seen in the failure of politicians to take responsibility for failures within their ministries and refusing to step down from office where abuses are unearthed. The problem with corruption and lack of accountability not only features in independent states but also in dependent territories as seen in the postponement of self-rule by Turks and Caicos in 2009 amidst allegations of systemic abuses in government. The lack of accountability is also clear where senior and mid-level risk averse bureaucrats find themselves implementing policies they do not support, understand and did not inform. A related issue is the need to improve public service ethics, especially among reform-fatigued personnel who have also undergone successive waves of salary freezes. It is clear however, that in the current dispensation of cost savings, governments will find it hard to address this issue via wage increase. Perhaps the solution is for the adoption of creative measures such as those undertaken in Jamaica.

A major challenge has been the emergence of dual and conflicting systems and culture in the public sector. For instance, even as automation is being encouraged, there remains a tendency to maintain old forms of accounting (e.g., notebooks) which ultimately undermine efficiency gains and sunk investments in new technology. This is also seen in the introduction of new and improved administrative practices and organizational forms alongside archaic ones. Here efforts at PSR have tended to be piecemeal, unconnected, subject to the turns of the electoral wheel or political expedience. In the case of the creation of executive agencies in countries such as Trinidad & Tobago and Jamaica, there is now an appearance of two public services with improvements not progressing across the entire public sector. The result is the overlaying of old structures and practices with new. This is so even as challenges have emerged around sustaining momentum in reformed entities, including executive agencies. Some of the challenges experienced have come from the adoption of externally motivated policies without attempt to tailor reforms to the local context.

To this end too, it is difficult to speak about governance capacity and human resources in the Caribbean context without mentioning migration. This is so given that the region has been noted as having the highest rates of migration of its most educated and skilled persons than any other in the world (Foner 1998; Minto-Coy 2009b). Over time this has amounted to a significant leakage of capital and resources given public investments in education and training. This group has evolved to become major partners for the region, with their support surpassing annual contributions of traditional international development partners as indicated (Minto-Coy 2016c, 2012, 2010). Surely, in light of the tremendous amount of skills in this group, their proven capacity in helping to bolster state capacity in vital areas such as education, health and the economy (tourism, investments and remittances) in countries such as Haiti, Jamaica, the Dominican Republic and Suriname (Minto-Coy 2016c, 2016d, 2010, 2009b; Seraphin 2015; Nurse 2004; Thomas-Hope 1998).

As noted earlier one of the important considerations in discussing public sector capacity is the extent to which the citizens are aware of shortfalls or demand more from their leaders. While it may be said that governance in the Caribbean has led to an expectation of poor performance among public sector leaders and underperformance in the public sector, the evidence still suggests desire among citizens for improvement. Certainly, the demonstrations in Guadeloupe and Martinique in 2009 were as much a result of the sense of exclusion of the black population from the governance of their own society as much as the resulting economic and social frustrations wrought by such exclusions (Minto-Coy and Berman 2016). Addressing these challenges will help to temper growing apathy, sustained migration of talent, crime, informality, and the lack of trust and support towards the state and its representatives.

Policy continuity and the willingness to work across party lines have been consistent themes, particularly in those independent territories. This has been fostered by the winner takes all political system and the battle over spoils and scarce benefits that typifies some resource weak setting. These remain worrying features particularly when an administration is changed. The FAO has for instance noted this as a lingering problem affecting trust and confidence in policies with emerging indications of a desire among some international partners to encourage local consensus on policies across political divides (Brown 2015). Again what becomes clear here is the major role that international development institutions have and can have in helping to improve the quality of governance in the Caribbean, a point supported more generally in the capacity development literature (Brusis 2003).

Conclusion: Good Enough Governance in Context

This chapter provides a framework for evaluating state sector capacity of nations. It defines this around four dimensions plus preconditions. These are accountability, a capable bureaucracy, resourcing and strategic leadership. For sure, the presence of other factors, termed societal factors, potentially constituting a fifth dimension has been acknowledged. The Caribbean has not been entirely successful or failing in these dimensions, a fact perhaps most illustrative in the region's rating as a grouping of mainly middle-income countries. Thus public sector capacity for development has been middling with middling results, reflective of a complex mix of legacy and contemporary issues.

The historical development shows a legacy of governance capacity that is weak in terms of its propensity to involve and seek consensus, that has fostered divisions between politics and bureaucracy, among different political groups, between government and the private sector, citizens and leaders, and finally along ethnic and class lines (IADB 2003). These have compromised the development and effect of public administration and policy across the region. Notwithstanding, the inherited institutions have helped to contribute to the region's fairly stable democracies with these helping to check the extent to which governments stray into poor governance. Modern day issues show development and progress, including the evolution in education, public sector reform and public financial management, as well as environmental and disaster risk management. Nonetheless, a number of weaknesses have been raised in the chapter.

The concluding paragraphs brings the reader back to the notion of good enough governance and implications for future capacity development. The approach taken here embraces the focus on policy and politics, the former drawing attention to government's performance in different policy areas and the latter to consensus and legitimacy (Capano, Howlett and Ramesh 2015). The concept also places context and institutional endowment in full view. Indeed, the call for good enough governance in this chapter does not suggest that better or best governance cannot be realized in the Caribbean. However, the preoccupation with the latter has been more in principle than reality.

The result has sometimes been precarious or unintended results (e.g., demoralization of the civil service), with policies being informed by external requirements, conditions, and models that have not taken contextual matters into account. Good enough governance means a conscious review of externally motivated reform agendas to see what aspects can be adopted and implemented over what period. Indeed, good enough governance also implies movement—improvement from one level of capacity to another. Within this is the notion of constant evolution and modification as informed by the previous achievements (and failures) as well as responsiveness to the changing dynamics and demands of the governance landscape (local, regional, and international, and citizen/clients). Good enough governance then, is a continuum en route to better governance with an understanding that governments (even the best) must continue to improve governance. This is important since the latter is not static and cannot be so in environments characterized by crises and change.

The term is also not in contention with the growing list of international indicators and best practice markers. Indeed, a focus on good enough governance within this perspective would force a more conscious consideration of the place of such international indicators in the local environment. GEG also suggests a more realistic assessment of where the Caribbean is in light of such indicators, the steps (immediate, long, and short-term) which need to be taken towards improvement and more realistic/honest markers and evaluations towards improved performance.

To this end, more flashes of public-spiritedness from leaders focused on improving their nations and willing to communicate across boundaries is critical. Likewise, the capacity-gaps in the public sector can be plugged by borrowing from other sectors (as seen in disaster management and the health sector). As such—and accepting that collaboration itself is not a cost-free policy approach—there is need for more engagement with the private sector, NGOs, and civil society in the delivery of public goods and services across the region. There is also a need to focus more on consistent and full implementation of reforms and the systematic collection and measurement of information on challenges and achievements of policy interventions. This will help to develop a local databank that can be drawn upon for more evidence-based policy making.

Indeed, there remains an urgency to mature governance across the Caribbean along the more realistic lines suggested by the GEG approach. In many ways, this is about achieving better governance and addressing some of the longstanding features of the public sector across the Caribbean. To this end, there remains a need for personnel management and organization practices to evolve to the demands of the Caribbean in the twenty-first century. Where reforms are being undertaken, there is need to understand what aspect of the public sector to reform and how remaining unchanged segments and culture can in fact stymy progress in the new. Ultimately, an understanding of what to reform is important but the governance of reform (i.e., the how) is just as important (Minto-Coy 2011b).

Strategic leadership at all levels of society (politics, bureaucracy, and private sector) will be important in advancing governance across the region in the ways suggested above. But so too is support from global development partners, willing to align influence *and money* with local leadership who take purposeful steps towards improving the public sector capacity. This latter point speaks directly to the reality of the region as a grouping of small developing states, highly linked and dependent on the international environment and funding support for achieving good enough governance. As noted earlier, governance costs and the need for international support will persist particularly given the interconnected and global nature of many emerging governance challenges (e.g., the Zika-virus). Having accepted this reality, the focus should be on determining what kind (e.g., technology, funds) and quantity of support is needed and in what policy areas so as to maximize the impact of such assistance.

As a vital member of the region's international development partners, marshalling the region's capacity for governance in the twenty-first century and beyond must mean the inclusion of its migrants and diaspora population—i.e., *transnational Caribbean*—as important stakeholders in regional and national development. Nevertheless, the aim remains to find the right balance in such relationships so as to prevent renewed dependencies and evolve sustainable governance regionally.

The evolution in the region's disaster management framework discussed above is one poignant example of the approach of good enough governance espoused in this chapter. Hence, the approach has been influenced by context and policy leaders learning over time and adapting measures to *do better* as it relates to environmental and disaster risk management. This emphasis on doing better has evolved into recognition that the state cannot unilaterally respond but that the involvement of diverse groups and communities through partnerships and inclusion is necessary at all levels of the policy process. Indeed, there may be specific challenges in other policy areas but this example as well as the still emerging developments in the Jamaican case, suggest the capacity among Caribbean countries for good enough governance for a sustainable Caribbean in the twenty-first century.

Notes

1. For example, islands such as Jamaica were ahead of Singapore in the early independence years but have fallen drastically since (Williams & Morgan, 2012).
2. Used here to refer mainly to Martinique, Guadeloupe, and their dependencies.

References

Bevir, M. (2012). *Governance: A Very Short Introduction*. Oxford: Oxford University Press.

Bissessar, Ann Marie (2002). "Introducing New Public Management in Caribbean Bureaucracies". In Ann Marie Bissessar (ed.), *Policy Transfer, New Public Management and Globalization*. Lanham, MD: University Press of America, pp. 135-153.

Blavy, Rodolphe (2006). "Public Debt and Productivity: The Difficult Quest for Growth in Jamaica", *IMF Working Paper, WP/06/235*.

Brown, Rudolph (2015). "UN Body Wants Continuity - FAO Pushing for Mature Governance from CARICOM States", *the Jamaica Gleaner*, December 14, 2015.   http://jamaica-gleaner.com/article/lead-stories/20151214/un-body-wants-continuity-fao-pushing-mature-governance-caricom-states

Bruhn, J. (2009). *In Search of Common Ground: Reconciling Western-based Governance Principles and First Nations Traditions*. Institute on Governance. http://iog.ca/wp-content/uploads/2012/12/2009_May_Traditions.pdf

Brusis, Martin (2003). "Developing Governance Capacity: A Review of Causes and Effects", Center for Applied Policy Research. Ceses.cuni.cz/CESES-136-version1-1E_Governance_Capacity_BTI_Brusis.pdf

Capano, Giliberto, Howlett, Michael and Ramesh, M (2015). *Varieties of Governance: Dynamics, Strategies, Capacities*, Basingstoke: Palgrave Macmillan, pp. 3–27.

CIPRA 2015. *Governance Capacity: Theoretical Concept*. (Schaan, Liechtenstein: Commission for the Protection of the Alps). http://alpsknowhow.cipra.org/main_topics/governance_capacity/governance_capacity_chapter_2.html

Fiorino, D. J. (2014). 21. "Sustainable Cities and Governance: What Are the Connections?" *Elgar Companion to Sustainable Cities: Strategies, Methods and Outlook*, 413. https://www.american.edu/spa/cep/up-load/fiorino_governance_7_26.pdf

Foner, Nancy (1998). "Towards a Comparative Perspective on Caribbean Migration" in Mary Chamberlain (Ed.) *Caribbean Migration: Globalised Identities*, London and New York: Routledge.

Food and Agriculture Organization of the United Nations (FAO) (2014). "FAO Caribbean Head Highlights Importance of Policy in Revitalizing Regional Agriculture", *FAO*, October 10. http://www.fao.org/americas/noticias/ver/en/c/260266/

Fukuyama, F. (2013). "*What Is Governance?*" CGD Working Paper 314. Washington, DC: Center for Global Development. http://www.cgdev.org/content/publications/detail/1426906

Gray, Obika (2004). *Demeaned but Empowered: The Social Power of the Urban Poor in Jamaica*, Jamaica, Barbados, and Trinidad and Tobago: University of the West Indies Press

Gindle, Merilee (2007). "Good Enough Governance Revisited", *Development Policy Review*, 25(5): 533–574.

——— (2004). "Good Enough Governance: Poverty Reduction and Reform in Developing Countries", *Governance*, 17(4): 525–548.

Harriott, Anthony (2008). *Organized Crime and Politics in Jamaica: Breaking the Nexus*, University of the West Indies: Canoe Press

Hertie School of Governance (2014). *The Governance Report 2014: Administrative Capacity and Governance Readiness*. (Berlin, Germany: Author). http://www.governancereport.org/home/governance-challenges/the-governance-report-2014/

Hufty, M. (2011). "Investigating policy processes: the governance analytical framework (GAF)." *Research for Sustainable Development: Foundations, Experiences, and Perspectives* (2011): 403–424.

Inter-American Development Bank (2003). Institutional Development Sector Facility Profile: Trinidad and Tobago. Public Sector Reform Preparation Program: Project Number TT-0057. IADB: Washington DC. June 6, 2003.

Jones, Edwin (1992). *Development Administration: Jamaican Adaptations*, Jamaica: CARICOM Publishers.

Linton, Latonya (2015). Improved Benefits for Public Sector Workers, August 14, 2015. Available at www.JIS.gov.jm/improved-benefits-for-public-sector-workers

Mills, Gladstone, E. (1997). "Westminster Style Democracy: The Jamaican Experience. Jamaica". *Grace Kennedy Foundation Lecture*. Kingston, Jamaica: The Grace Kennedy Foundation.

Minto-Coy, Indianna (2016a). "The History of Public Administration in the Commonwealth Caribbean", *Public Administration and Policy in the Caribbean*, Indianna D. Minto-Coy and Evan Berman (eds), Boca Raton, London, New York: CRC Press, pp. 33–60.

_____ (2016b). "Policy and Regulation of the Caribbean Communications Industry", *Public Administration and Policy in the Caribbean*, Indianna D. Minto-Coy and Evan Berman (eds), Boca Raton, London, New York: CRC Press, pp. 357–378.

_____ (2016c). "Diaspora Engagement for Development in the Caribbean", *Diasporas, Development and Governance*, Abel Chikanda et al. (eds), Switzerland: Springer, pp. 121–139.

_____ (2016d). "The Role of Diasporas in the Growth and Internationalization of Businesses from Countries of Origin", *Diaspora Business*, Maria Elo and Liesl Riddle (eds), Oxford: Inter-Disciplinary.Net

_____ (2011a). "Social Partnerships and Development: Lessons for the Caribbean", *Caribbean Papers No 12*, Waterloo, Canada: Centre for International Governance Innovation.

_____ (2011b). *Towards Public Sector Reforms in Jamaica: What Can Local and International Experiences Tell Us About Successful Public Sector Reform*, Kingston, Jamaica: CAPRI.

_____ (2009a). *The Role of Incumbent Firms in Regulatory Reform: The Case of Ireland and Jamaica*, PhD Thesis, Law Department, London School of Economics and Political Sciences.

_____ (2009b). "Diasporas and Development: Lessons from Ireland and the Caribbean", *Caribbean Paper No 11*, Waterloo, Canada: Centre for International Governance Innovation

Minto-Coy, Indianna and Berman, Evan (2016). *Public Administration and Policy in the Caribbean*, Boca Raton, London, New York: CRC Press.

Nurse, Keith (2004). "Diaspora, Migration and Development in the Caribbean", *FOCAL Policy Paper*, Ontario: FOCAL.

OCED (2015a). *Towards A Framework for the Governance of Public Infrastructure*. (Paris, France: OECD). http://www.oecd.org/officialdocuments/publicdisplaydocumentpdf/?cote=GOV/PGC/SBO(2015)6anddocLanguage=En

_____ (2015b). *Government at a Glance 2015*. http://www.oecdilibrary.org/docserver/download/4215081e.pdf?expires=1446072455andid=idandaccname=guestandchecksum=F88284271C3B3C3F74C45D216FB9B7C8

Sampson, Cezley I. (1996). "Jamaica: Public Enterprise Reform", *Policy Reform for Sustainable Development in the Caribbean*, Michele Garrity and Louis A. Picard (eds), Amsterdam/Brussels: IOS Press/International Institute of Administrative Sciences-IIAS.

Seraphin, Hugues (2015). "Marketing and Tourism: Research Method for the Segmentation of the Haitian Diaspora", *Conference of the International Journal of Arts and Sciences*, 08(02): 147–154.

Sutton, Paul (2008). "Public Sector Reform in the Commonwealth Caribbean: A Review of Recent Experiences", *Caribbean Paper No. 6*, October 2008, Waterloo, Canada: Caribbean Economic Governance Program.

Thomas-Hope, Elizabeth (1998a). 'Return Migration to Jamaica and its Development Potential', *International Migration* 37(1): 183–204.

United Nations (2011). *Towards Human Resilience: Sustaining MDG Progress in an Age of Economic Uncertainty: Governance Principles, Institutional Capacity and Quality* (chapter 8). (New York: UN). http://www.undp.org/content/dam/undp/library/Poverty%20Reduction/Inclusive%20development/Towards%20Human%20Resilience/Towards_SustainingMDGProgress_Ch8.pdf

_____ (2011). *Measuring Change in Institutional Performance, Adaptability and Stability*. http://www.undp.org/content/dam/undp/library/Poverty%20Reduction/Inclusive%20development/Towards%20Human%20Resilience/Towards_SustainingMDGProgress_Ch8.pdf

Wallace, Elisabeth (1977). *The British Caribbean: Form the Decline of Colonialism to the End of Federation*, Toronto, Canada: Toronto University Press.

Williams, Densil and Morgan, Beverley (2012). *Competitiveness of Small Nations: What Matters?* Kingston, Jamaica: Arawak Publishers.

World Bank (1992). *Governance and Development*, Washington, D.C.: World Bank.

_____ (1994). *Governance. The World Bank's Experience.* Washington D.C.: World Bank. https://books.google.co.nz/books/about/Governance.html?id=lylQWqEdtrkCandredir_esc=y

_____ (1996). *Jamaica: Public Sector Modernization Project*, Washnigton, D.C.: World Bank.

_____ (2015). *Worldwide Governance Indicators (WGI) Project.* http://info.worldbank.org/governance/wgi/index.aspx#home

CHAPTER 4

Reforming Education in the Caribbean

From Policy to Transformative Leadership

Denise Pearson

Summary

Chapter 4 claims that Caribbean systems of education experience some of the same multi-dimensional challenges as many of its global neighbors. According to the author, educational leaders and policy makers in the Caribbean should consider the thinking of certain scholars who advocate for critical theory approaches to leadership, which can effectively address these challenges.

> Education, the beyond all other devices of human origin, is the great equalizer of the conditions of men, the balance wheel of the social machinery (Horace Mann 1848).

Introduction

The effectiveness of government-sponsored education in the Caribbean is the subject of concern for a wide range of stakeholders, including local and regional education organizations, and governmental and nongovernmental entities. The region joins other nations who are critically examining the role and impact of these systems on achieving national goals and improving the human condition of its citizens. Quality of life, economic development, and viable democracies are inextricably linked to effective systems of education. In 1954, Chief Justice of the United States affirmed the critical role of education in the country's democracy when he rendered the following ruling in the landmark U.S. Supreme Court case, Brown vs. the Board of Education:

> Today, education is perhaps the most important function of state and local governments. Compulsory school attendance and the great expenditures for education both demonstrate our recognition of the importance of education to our democratic society. It is required in the performance of our most basic public responsibilities, even service in the armed forces. It is the very foundation of good citizenship.[1]

Furthermore, there is evidence for concern given disparities in individual and group educational experiences despite decades of efforts to reform, and in some cases transform, ineffective systems.

Education policy makers expend enormous amounts of resources—human and financial—engaged in policy development aimed at improving educational systems, with increasing focus on student learning outcomes. Nonetheless, that state of education in many places around the globe is in crisis, which is characterized by, but not limited to issues related to teacher quality, student readiness for postsecondary education, and educational equity. The notion of equity is differentiated from the concept of equity, as it necessarily attributes responsibility to organizational structures that give birth to and nurture educational disparities. As such, policy makers are encouraged to specifically consider education reform efforts from a structural framework.

In response to persistent concerns which threaten the economic health of communities around the world, policy makers continue to identify relevant problems that continue to challenge systems of education, including their impact on the students they serve. In consultation with a wide range of stakeholders, research is ongoing, policy alternatives are generated, adopted, and assessed for impact. Despite policy formulation developed to improve educational outcomes for learners, problems and inequities persist, which leads to a different path of examination—namely leadership. Transformative leadership for education reform in the Caribbean is the focus of this discussion. Psychologists Coby and Damon (2009) have been quoted as saying, "The course of society is largely determined by the quality of its moral leadership" (p. 69). Transformative leadership that leads to sustainable and effective educational reform in the Caribbean may also be determined by the quality of its moral leadership.[2]

The Caribbean is part of a far reaching phenomenon that highlights systems of education that fall short of quality education for all of its citizens. The region is joined with other political economies around the globe, as it continues to examine the juxtaposition of education, politics, and democracy. In 1990 delegates from more than 150 countries joined with representatives from nearly 150 governmental and nongovernmental agencies for the World Conference on Education for All (March 5–9), in Jomtien, Thailand. The aim of the conference was to make primary education accessible to all children and to massively reduce illiteracy before the end of the decade (UNESCO).[3] At the conference, delegates adopted a World Declaration on Education for All, and reaffirmed the idea that education is a fundamental human right. The goals for the subsequent Framework for Action to Meet the Basic Learning Needs by the year 2000 were clearly articulated to include universal access to learning; a focus on equity; emphasis on learning outcomes; broadening the means and the scope of basic education; enhancing the environment for learning; and strengthening partnerships by 2000.

In 2000, governments from 164 countries came together in Dakar, Senegal, for the World Education Forum and reported on the results of Education for All efforts since 1990. Miller (2014) asserts that the vision for the Education for All declaration was "simple and powerful"—affirming the right of all children, youth, and adults to be afforded educational opportunities that meet their basic learning needs (p. 1). Referencing the Caribbean specifically, Miler asserts that Universal Primary Education has been a focus of Caribbean governments for many years, at least rhetorically, and agrees with evaluation of Education for All efforts which have been described as falling short of their goals as summarized in UNESCO's EFA Summary Report (EFA Global Monitoring Report 2015).[4]

In response to problems plaguing their system of education and similar to other regions of the world, the Caribbean has engaged in multiple attempts to reform education over the course of the past two decades. Failed efforts caused Jules (2014) to revisit the question, what is the purpose of education in the Caribbean? Jules asserts that many of such unsuccessful reform initiatives amounted to projects promoted by multilaterals and benefactor organizations in accordance with established paradigms. Jules recognizes the implications of the internalization of education in a globalized world, and notes the shift in the guiding questions from what should be taught to what are the skills and competencies required for any area of knowledge?

The future of education in the Caribbean should not be discussed in isolation of a guiding philosophy according to Jules, and the Statement of the Ideal Caribbean (CARCOM) Person and the UNESCO Imperatives for Learning in the 21st Century, which were presented for inclusion in education reform discussions. The philosophical foundations for the ideal CARCOM person are: love life; emotionally intelligent; environmentally sensitive; democratically engaged; culturally grounded and historically conscious; multiple literacies; gender and diversity respectful; and entrepreneurial capable.[5] As transformational leaders identify the next phase of educational reform efforts, this cultural context may support relevance and sustainability.

The Caribbean's Diverse Landscape

The Caribbean has been defined differently over history as being comprised of Dutch-, English-, French-, and Spanish-speaking territories, as

Table 4.1 *Countries of the Caribbean (also known as the West Indies and the Antilles) arranged by official language*

English	Dutch	French	Spanish
Anguilla	Aruba	Haiti*	Cuba
Antigua & Barbuda	Curacao	Guadeloupe	Dominican
The Bahamas	Dutch Caribbean:	Martinique	Republic
Barbados	Saba, Bonaire, and	French Guiana	Puerto Rico
Belize	St. Eustatius	*** Haitian Creole**	
Bermuda	St. Maarten (also	Official language	
British Virgin Islands	English-official)	of Haiti	
Cayman Islands	Suriname		
Dominica			
Grenada	*** Papiamento**		
Guyana	(Portuguese &		
Jamaica	Spanish-based		
Montserrat	Creole language)		
St. Kitts & Nevis	Official language of		
St. Lucia	Aruba, Bonaire, and		
St. Vincent & Grenadines	Curacao		
Trinidad & Tobago			
Turks & Caicos Islands			
U.S. Virgin Islands			

Source: Society for Caribbean Linguistics. http://www.scl-online.net/FAQS/caribbean.htm . Retrieved June 22, 2015.

Figure 4.1 Map of the Caribbean

Source: World Atlas. http://www.worldatlas.com/webimage/countrys/carib.htm . Retrieved June 20, 2015.

illustrated in Table 4.1. Figure 4.1 provides a geographical illustration of the region, which consists of 31 distinct political entities.

The Caribbean as Global Partner in Pursuit of Education for All

For the Caribbean, the United States and elsewhere around the globe, education remains a key strategy towards upward mobility and economic strength. As the world becomes "flat" and increasingly interdependent, and as geographical lines are being erased, both literally and figuratively, shared global concerns around the notion of an educated citizenry cross lines of sovereignty. The Caribbean need only look a relatively short distance to its North American relative to witness shared concerns and equally robust calls for educational reform, which have been underway for decades with the goal of promoting student achievement and strengthening global competitive position through educational excellence and ensuring equal access. Although education is primarily a State and local responsibility in the US, the federal government has a significant role in its provision to citizens, and overall educational reform.

Errol Miller has written extensively on the subject of education in this region of the world (1992, 1994, and 2010; www.mord.mona.uwi.edu/staff/view.asp?pid=10227). Miller notes that despite political dependency,

British influence on education in the Caribbean has diminished significantly since the late 1950s. He further asserts North America's growing influence in this area, which was one impetus for this writing that is somewhat comparative in nature. Given that assertion, it may be instructive to offer brief comparisons and contrasts between the two regions.

Like the United States, the Commonwealth Caribbean provides free public education to its citizens up to 15–17 years of age, depending on the territory. Miller (1999) acknowledges that there are similarities in the challenges confronting Caribbean and U.S. systems of education. With regard to education reform, he makes the point that the Commonwealth Caribbean (also commonly referred to as "English-speaking Caribbean" is comparable to more developed countries in their provision of education to its population. (Commonwealth Caribbean Education in the Global Context, p. 4). In common with other developing and developed nations, the Commonwealth Caribbean and its citizens recognize education as providing the greatest assurance for socioeconomic advancement. In the US, for example, the relationship between education, income disparity, and unemployment is clear. Simply stated, the more education one attains, the more income they accrue and the less likely they are to be unemployed (see Tables 4.2 and 4.3 for illustration).

In the United States, social policy discussions, widespread education reform initiatives, and grassroots activism are converging with increasing focus on quality of education for all citizens with an emphasis on equity. Although the purpose of education is still debated in some societies and

Table 4.2 Mean earnings by highest degree earned in dollars: 2009

Education Level	Mean Earnings in U.S. Dollars
Doctorate	103,000
Professional	128,000
Master's	74,000
Bachelor's	57,000
Associate's	40,000
Some college/no degree	32,000
High school graduate only	31,000
Not a high school graduate	20,000
All	42,000

Table 4.3 Unemployment rates by educational attainment:
percentage (US Bureau of Labor Statistics)

Year	Less than High School	College and Above
2006	6.8	2.0
2007	7.1	2.0
2008	9.0	2.6
2009	14.7	4.6
2010	14.9	4.7
2011	14.3	4.3

Source: Statistical Abstract of the United States, published by the U.S. Census Bureau.

countries, Huitt has identified three primary purposes of education, which include the development of one's purpose in life, the development of one's character, and the development of competence.[6] The economic and social impacts of an educated citizenry correlates with a productive citizenry.

In the 1954, the United States landmark Brown vs. the Board of Education case, the Supreme Court ruled that, "Segregation of students in public schools violates the Equal Protection Clause of the Fourteenth Amendment, because separate facilities are inherently unequal." (Oliver Brown, et al. v Board of Education of Topeka, et al., 347 U.S. 483 (1954). More than fifty years later, there is renaissance movement of sorts to reposition the concept of equality in education at the top of political, social, and community agendas in the agenda. This is discussed in the edited book, *Quality Education as a Constitutional Right* (Perry, Moses, et al. 2010), which presents a serious appeal for the transformation of public education in America. With historical foundations, the authors present a cogent and compelling argument for youth involvement, the role of U.S. Constitution, and the unwavering pursuit of educational excellence for all citizens, as the prerequisites for real and sustainable transformation.[7]

Under the auspices of the U.S. Education Department, policy discussions and legislation focus on the promotion of student achievement, educational excellence, and equality on behalf of national security persists. The very mission of the Education Department is to "promote student achievement and preparation for global competitiveness by fostering educational excellence and ensuring equal access." Established in 1980 by combining offices from several federal agencies, the Department of Education employs more than 4000 employees and has a $68 billion budget to set policies on federal financial aid for education, and distributing as well as monitoring those funds; collecting data on America's schools and disseminating research; focusing national attention on key educational issues; and prohibiting discrimination and ensuring equal access to education.[8]

No Child Left Behind (NCLB) Act was signed into U.S. law in 2002, which mandated standards-based education to improve student achievement. The Act required states to develop assessments in basic skills to qualify for federal school funding. The Act does not assert a national achievement standard, which is left up to individual states to develop their own standards. This perpetuates inequality in education. This expanded federal role in public education involves annual testing, annual academic progress, report cards, teacher qualifications, and funding changes.

NCLB Act requires all public schools receiving federal funding to administer a state-wide standardized test annually to all students. This means that all students take the same test under the same conditions. Schools that receive Title I funding through the Elementary and Secondary Education Act of 1965 must make adequate yearly progress (AYP) in test scores. If the school's results are repeatedly poor, subsequent steps are required to be taken to improve the school. The Act also requires states to provide highly qualified teachers to all students, although each state sets its own standards for what counts as highly qualified. Similarly, the act requires states to set "one high, challenging standard" for its students, and these curriculum standards must be applied to all students, rather than having different standards for students in different cities or parts of the state—which, in its absence, results in inequitable systems of education.

To address failed policies, persistent achievement disparities between low and high wealth communities, and the complexity of education in a diverse twenty-first century global society, the U.S. has implemented other targeted educational policy initiatives including the White House Initiative on Educational Excellence for African Americans; White House Initiative on Educational Excellence for Hispanics; White House Initiative on Asian Americans and Pacific Islanders; White House Initiative on Historically Black Colleges and Universities; and White House Initiative on American Indian and Alaska Native Education.[9]

In response to disappointing results of NCLB, a recent movement to reform public education in the U.S. involves the notion of a Common Core, which is comprised of a set of national standards that aim to replace the wide range of individual state standards, address concerns involving teacher preparation, reform instruction, and change systems of assessment and accountability. Despite this and other large-scale efforts to improve systems of education, educational leaders, policy makers, and other stakeholders recognize that a strong Common Core and other targeted strategies are not enough to address persistent and systemic problems that challenge the future of the developed world. Increasingly, the focus is being shifted to educator and leader preparation.

In comparison, the Caribbean has its own compelling narrative and history of actions aimed at education reform, of which many parallel concerns and efforts are underway in other parts of the globe. As is the case in other nations, the Caribbean is beginning to increase its focus on outputs as opposed to a myopic focus on inputs. Education inputs include such variables as school autonomy, school choice, funding, pupil-teacher ratios, and years in school. Outputs include cognitive skills (learning as measured by standardized tests) and other educational outcomes including graduation rates, literacy, and employment. While outputs are important measures of educational effectiveness, policy makers are cautioned against relying too heavily on these measures. Much of outputs that are measured represent only part of why public education exists. Specifically, public schools also serve to promote the goals of civic responsibility, cultural awareness, personal freedom, and self-sufficiency. Acknowledging the validity of inputs in educational policy and reform conversations may lead to more comprehensive reform efforts as it considers the role of other factors in student achievement such as structural social, economic, and educational variables. (Rice 2015).[10]

The Organization of Eastern Caribbean States (OECS), the Caribbean Community (CARICOM), and Ministries of Education collaborated in 1991 to develop their Education Reform Strategy in concert with other significant international and regional education reform efforts. The OECS is comprised of nine states that include Antigua and Barbuda; Anguilla; British Virgin Islands; St. Kitts and Nevis; Montserrat; St. Vincent and the Grenadines; Commonwealth of the Dominican Republic; Grenada; and St. Lucia.

Using conventional policy generative methods, the OECS undertook a strategic process that began with an analysis of the region's education systems, interacted with chief education officers of the OECS countries, consulted with a broad cross-section of stakeholders in each country, and conducted extensive research including literature reviews before making any policy recommendations. An OECS Education Reform Strategy emerged and included the following strategies aimed at improving educational outcomes in the region:

1. Strategies for Harmonizing the Education Systems or the OECS
2. Strategies for Reforming Early Childhood Education
3. Strategies for Reforming Primary Education
4. Strategies for Reforming Secondary Education
5. Strategies for Reforming Tertiary, Continuing, and Adult Education
6. Strategies for Reforming the Terms and Conditions of Service for Teachers
7. Strategies for Reforming the Management and Administration of the Education System
8. Strategies for Reforming the Financing of Education
9. Strategies for the Reform Process [11]

Educational Leadership for Transformation

As this contribution is largely concerned with the intersection of educational reform and leadership, it is useful to take a closer look at OECS's Strategies for Reforming the Management and Administration of the Education System in particular. The rationale for the strategy takes the position that the management and administration of education within free, open, and democratic societies should both reflect and advance the precepts and ideals of freedom and democracy in the Caribbean. In concurrence with conventional approaches to sustainable change and reform efforts, the management and administration of education should be characterized by shared decision making that includes broad representation; continuous discourse and consultation among stakeholders; intermittent discussion and re-negotiation of goals, mission, and methodologies; full access to public information; provision for leadership capacity building

and a climate for the self-actualization of individuals, which would include adequate and appropriate training in management and administration for school personnel, and comprehensive public accountability.[12]

To move beyond policy implementation and toward transformational
leadership for sustainable reform, management and administration will
be compelled to transcend transactional leadership thinking and acting,
which generally aim to keep systems running with lesser focus on strategic visioning, which may also involve taking risks. In contrast, transformational leaders engage in thought and action that can lead to radical
change—to effectively address the challenges of education in the Caribbean in the twenty-first century. Educational leaders who seek to move
beyond policy to transform their schools, communities, and region, are
increasingly focusing on the notions of collaboration with an unwavering
commitment to high performance teams that foster high levels of student
learning and structural effectiveness and efficiency.

The impact of leadership on student learning has long been a domain
of interest for educators, policy makers, and other stakeholder groups. It is
limiting to think education reform efforts begin and end with policy formation. Letihwood, Louis, et al. (2004) examined the influence of leadership on student learning and asserted two noteworthy claims: 1. leadership
is second only to classroom instruction among all school-related factors
that foster student learning in school, and 2. the effects of leadership are
generally most significant where and when they are needed most. Their
research findings have implications for educational reform in the Caribbean as they advocate for moving beyond "models" of leadership to affect
school change. Instructive for educational reform in the Caribbean, they
promote leadership agility that considers organizational context and the
students it serves. Leithwood, Loius, et al. also consider the policy context,
which is necessarily at the nucleus of large-scale educational reform efforts.

The prevalence of a leadership-learning connection is accepted by
many, however the Learning from Leadership Project (Leithwood, Louis
et al. 2004) provides evidence of how leadership influences student
achievement. The project reminds education reformers of the indirect
impact of leaders on learners through their influence on people and the
organizational environment. It not only supports notions of educational
priorities that include teachers, but also highlights the importance of the

internal and external professional community. Finally, the project acknowledges the need to discover more about what leaders do in addition to the nature and influence of those behaviors and practices.[13]

To create and sustain transformative systems of education in the Caribbean (and beyond) will require deliberate actions at the systems and local levels. Investment in leadership development needs to be part of policy implementation strategies as there are specific leadership competencies needed to transform systems and organizations. Widespread evidence supports the position that effective educational leaders possess personal qualities that foster a culture of excellence for all students under their auspices. To that end, they believe and communicate that all students can achieve at high levels and hold themselves and others accountable for student success. Transformative leaders are evidence-driven and use data to set goals and achieve student learning. Transformative leaders leverage their deep knowledge of curriculum, instruction, and assessment to improve student learning and align strategies accordingly. They have a unique ability to develop staff, share leadership, and build strong school communities. They additionally know how to effectively manage resources and operations to advance student learning outcomes.

Early studies examining the nexus of educational leadership and transformation include the work of Murphy (1994), which highlights the critical role of principals in promoting the success of teachers; shared governance and decision making; cultivating strategic relationships; facilitating the creation of a shared vision; allocating resources in alignment with the shared vision; providing information for teacher empowerment; facilitating the professional development of teachers; and managing educational reform.[14] Leithwood and Jantzi (1999) researched the effects of transformational leadership on organizational climate and student engagement. Their study included survey data from more than 1,700 teachers and nearly 10,000 students. The study explored the concept of transformational leadership in school contexts which described it as representing the transcendence of self-interest by the leader and his/her followers.[15] The researchers developed a model of transformational leadership using six domains: building school vision and goals; providing intellectual stimulation; offering individualized support; symbolizing professional practices and values; demonstrating high performance expectations; and developing structures to foster participation in school decisions.

The definition of transformative leadership as offered by Bennis' (1959) definition of transformative leadership as one's ability to "reach the souls of others in a fashion which raises human consciousness, builds meanings and inspires human intent that is the source of power" (Dillard 1995: 560).[16] The Caribbean is positioned to join her global neighbors in authentic and contextually-based efforts to transform education in the region. Bold and less-fearful leadership in policy, governmental and nongovernmental arenas will be required, however, to develop and implement meaningful policies.

Conclusion

If, as Horace Mann asserted in 1848 education is the balance wheel of societies, a new kind of selfless and forward-thinking leadership will be needed. Welner and Carter's (2013) describe an "opportunity gap" indicator to reframe how educational leaders, policy makers and others should examine educational inequities.[17] Government leadership can address structural issues, including the development and support of teachers, by investing in the preparation of effective school leadership. Quality school leadership is particularly relevant in high-poverty communities where leadership stability may have an even greater impact. This type of leadership is necessarily deliberate in its aims to close the opportunity and achievement gaps, which are said to be interrelated. This type of leadership is also critical and may be contrary to convention.

Caribbean educational leaders and policy makers should consider the thinking of certain management and leadership scholars who advocate for critical theory approaches to leadership, which Western (2008) discusses through the four lenses of 1. emancipation; 2. depth analysis, 3. looking awry; and 4. systemic praxis.[18] Western defines a critical approach to leadership as:

- looking for new possibilities and positive implications for social action;
- providing critical account of historical and cultural conditions;
- engaging in critical re-examination of the conceptual frameworks used; and

- confronting alternative social explanation through analysis of their strengths and weaknesses, but then illustrating capacity to synthesize and incorporate their insights to strengthen their critical foundations (p. 9).

Caribbean systems of education are experiencing some of the same challenges as many of its global neighbors. In particular, some communities are struggling with serious issues of access and equity, which will require new approaches to policy making and implementation, in particular leadership. What has been offered is additional ways to engage in a serious discussion that has serious implications for a growing region.

Notes

1. Supreme Court of the United States, Brown v. Board of Education (347 U.S. 483), 3. In Perry, T, Moses, R.P., et al. (2010). *Quality Education as a Constitutional Right*. Boston, MA: Beacon Press. (p. 99).
2. Johnson, C. (2009). *Meeting the Ethical Challenges of Leadership*. Thousand Oaks, CA: SAGE Publications. (p. 69).
3. 2000 World Conference on Education for All. *UNESCO EFA Global Monitoring Report*. www.unsco.org. Retrieved July 15, 2015.
4. Miller, Paul. (2014). Education for All in the Caribbean: promise, paradox and possibility. *Research in Comparative and International Education* 9, November, pp. 1–3.
5. Jules, D. (2010). Rethinking Education in the Caribbean. *Caribbean Examinations Council*. www.cxc.org. Retrieved June 18, 2015.
6. Huitt, W. (2004). *Moral and Character Development*.
7. Perry, T., Moses, R.P., Wynne, J.T., Cortes, Jr., E., and Delpit, L (2010). Editors. *Quality Education as a Constitutional Right*. Boston, MA: Beacon Press.
8. United States Department of Education. www.ed.gov . Retrieved March 10, 2015.
9. The United States Department of Education. www.ed.gov/about/inits/list/index.html. Retrieved February 28, 2015.
10. Rice, J.K. (2015). *Investing in Equal Opportunity: What Would it Take to Build a Balancing Wheel*. National Education Policy Center. School of Education: University of Colorado Boulder.
11. The Organization of Eastern Caribbean States. www.oesc.org . Retrieved January 10, 2015.

12. Ibid.
13. Letihwood, K., Louis, K.S., Anderson, S. and Wahlstrom, K. (2004). *Research on How Leadership Influences Student Learning*. The Wallace Foundation.
14. Murphy, J. (1994). Transformational Change and the Evolving Role of the Principal: Early Empirical Research. AERA, April 1994. ERIC Document Number ED 374 520, pp. 1–50.
15. Leithwood, K. and Jantzi, D. (1999). The Effects of Transformational Leadership on Organizational Conditions and Student Engagement with School. Paper presented at the Annual Meeting of the American Educational Research Association (Montreal, Quebec, Canada, April 19–23). ERIC ED 432 035, 34 p.
16. Dillard, C.B. (1995). Leading with Her Life: An African-American Feminist (re)-Interpretation of Leadership for an Urban High School Principal." *School Effectiveness and School Improvement* 31(4): 539–563.
17. Welner, K.G. & Carter, P.L. (2013). Achievement Gaps Arise from Opportunity Gaps. In Closing the Achievement Gap: What America Must Do to Give Every Child a Chance, P.L. Carter & K.G. Welner (eds), NY: Oxford University Press.
18. Western, S. (2008). *Leadership: A Critical Text*. Los Angeles, CA: SAGE Publications.

About the Contributors

Evan M. Berman is a professor of public management and director of internationalization at the Victoria University of Wellington (New Zealand) School of Government. He is a distinguished Fulbright scholar, senior editor of *Public Performance and Management Review*, and founding editor of the American Society for Public Administration's book series on public administration and public policy. Berman has widely published in all of the major journals of the discipline. His related books in this series include *Public Administration in East Asia*, *Public Administration in Southeast Asia*, and *Public Administration in South Asia*. His areas of expertise include public performance and human resource management, and he is a co-author of the leading textbook *Human Resource Management in Public Service* as well as *Essential Statistics for Public Managers and Policy Analysts*.

Nikolaos Karagiannis is Professor of Economics at Winston-Salem State University, North Carolina, and the co-editor of the journal *American Review of Political Economy* (ARPE). He has authored, co-authored, and co-edited 18 books, and has published over 70 papers in scholarly journals and edited books, and over 60 short papers and articles in newspapers, magazines, and electronic media sources in the areas of economic development, public sector economics, and macroeconomic policy analysis. Karagiannis is particularly interested in Developmental State theory and policy, and his research has focused extensively on the applicability of this interventionist perspective in different contexts such as EU countries, the United States, Caribbean small island economies, and North African countries. His latest books include *The U.S. Economy and Neoliberalism: Alternative Strategies and Policies* (hardcover and paperback), and *Europe in Crisis: Problems, Challenges, and Alternative Perspectives*.

Zagros Madjd-Sadjadi is Professor of Economics at Winston-Salem State University. He is the former Chief Economist of the City and County of San Francisco and was a Lecturer in the Department of Economics at The University of the West Indies, Mona in Kingston, Jamaica from 2003 to 2006. The former President of the Southern Association for Canadian Studies in the United States, Madjd-Sadjadi has published extensively in the history of economic thought, political economy, and law and economics, including two books through Business Expert Press on *The Economics of Civil and Common Law and The Economics of Crime.*

Indianna D. Minto-Coy is a Senior Research Fellow at the Mona School of Business and Management, University of the West Indies, Jamaica. She is also a research affiliate at the International Migration Research Centre at Wilfrid Laurier University, Canada. Minto-Coy has held appointments at the Skoll Centre for Social Entrepreneurship at the Said Business School of the University of Oxford, the University of Waterloo, the Centre for International Governance Innovation (where she also coordinated the research component of the Caribbean Economic Governance Project), and the Shridath Ramphal Centre for Trade Policy, Law and Services, University of the West Indies, Barbados. Minto-Coy's work spans areas of public policy, ICTs, migration and diasporas, and entrepreneurship. She holds a PhD (Law) from the London School of Economics and Political Sciences.

Debbie A. Mohammed obtained her PhD from the University of the West Indies in 2005. She is a Senior Lecturer in International Trade at the Institute of International Relations and the Arthur Lok Jack Graduate School of Business, the University of the West Indies, Trinidad and Tobago and one of five members of the EU-LAC Academic Council. She is the author of one book and has published extensively in academic journals and contributed book chapters to several important scholarly works in the areas of Caribbean economic development, competitiveness, regional economic integration, and trade facilitation. Her current research focuses on culture and governance as transformative factors for socioeconomic development. Mohammed uses Twitter and Facebook to advance specific issues relating to governance and development.

Denise Pearson has worked in the higher education community for more than 20 years. She is currently employed at Winston-Salem State University as senior associate dean of the College of Arts, Sciences, Business and Education, and Professor of Education. Prior to joining Winston-Salem State University, Pearson worked at the University of Denver, School of Continuing and Professional Studies, as associate dean. Pearson's research interests involve issues related to organizational leadership and conflict management, with an emphasis on higher education and historically black colleges and universities (HBCUs). In 2006, she was hosted as a visiting professor in the Conflict Management Program at the Nelson Mandela Metropolitan University in Port Elizabeth, South Africa. She also worked collaboratively on a U.S. Department of Education grant between the University of Denver and the University of the West Indies to build conflict-resolution capacity in Trinidad & Tobago communities. Pearson received a PhD in Administration and Supervision of Education from Marquette University, MA in Conflict Resolution from the University of Denver, MS in Education Administration from Concordia University, and BA in Human Services from Pace University.

C. J. Polychroniou is a political economist/political scientist who has taught and worked in universities and research centers in Europe and the United States. His main research interests are in European economic integration, globalization, the political economy of the United States, and the deconstruction of neoliberalism's politico-economic project. He is a regular contributor to Al Jazeera and Truthout as well as a member of Truthout's Public Intellectual Project. He has published several books and his articles have appeared in a variety of journals, magazines, newspapers, and popular news websites. Many of his publications have been translated into several foreign languages, including Croatian, French, Greek, Italian, Portuguese, Spanish, and Turkish.

Index

OTHER TITLES FROM THE ECONOMICS COLLECTION

Philip Romero, The University of Oregon and
Jeffrey Edwards, North Carolina A&T State University, *Editors*

- *U.S. Politics and the American Macroeconomy* by Gerald T. Fox
- *Seeing the Future: How to Build Basic Forecasting Models* by Tam Bang Vu
- *The Economics of Civil and Common Law* by Zagros Madjd-Sadjadi
- *Innovative Pricing Strategies to Increase Profits, Second Edition* by Daniel Marburger
- *Business Liability and Economic Damages* by Scott Gilbert
- *How Strong is Your Firm's Competitive Advantage, Second Edition* by Daniel Marburger
- *Eastern European Economies: A Region in Transition* by Marcus Goncalves and Erika Cornelius Smith
- *Health Financing Without Deficits: Reform That Sidesteps Political Gridlock* by Philip Romero and Randy Miller
- *Central and Eastern European Economies: Perspectives and Challenges* by Marcus Goncalves and Erika Cornelius Smith
- *Regression for Economics, Second Edition* by Shahdad Naghshpour
- *A Primer on Nonparametric Analysis: Volume I* by Shahdad Naghshpour
- *A Primer on Nonparametric Analysis: Volume II* by Shahdad Naghshpour
- *The Modern Caribbean Economy, Volume II: Economic Development and Public Policy Challenges* edited by Nikolaos Karagiannis and Debbie A. Mohammed

Announcing the Business Expert Press Digital Library

Concise e-books business students need for classroom and research

This book can also be purchased in an e-book collection by your library as

- *a one-time purchase,*
- *that is owned forever,*
- *allows for simultaneous readers,*
- *has no restrictions on printing, and*
- *can be downloaded as PDFs from within the library community.*

Our digital library collections are a great solution to beat the rising cost of textbooks. E-books can be loaded into their course management systems or onto students' e-book readers.
The **Business Expert Press** digital libraries are very affordable, with no obligation to buy in future years. For more information, please visit **www.businessexpertpress.com/librarians.**
To set up a trial in the United States, please email **sales@businessexpertpress.com**.

www.ingramcontent.com/pod-product-compliance
Lightning Source LLC
Chambersburg PA
CBHW071448200326
41519CB00019B/5658